webpage crea...

Unit 20
creating animation for the WWW using ICT

Graham Manson
Anne Kelsall
Ruksana Patel
Steve Cushing
Consultant: Keith Parry

OCR level
Nationals

ict

www.payne-gallway.co.uk

✓ Free online support
✓ Useful weblinks
✓ 24 hour online ordering

01865 888070

PAYNE-GALLWAY

Payne-Gallway is an imprint of Pearson Education Limited, a company incorporated in England and Wales, having its registered office at Edinburgh Gate, Harlow, Essex, CM20 2JE. Registered company number: 872828

www.payne-gallway.co.uk

Text © Graham Manson 2007

First published 2007

12 11 10 09
10 9 8 7 6 5 4

British Library Cataloguing in Publication Data is available from the British Library on request.

ISBN 978 1 905292 14 1

Edited by Liz Cartmell
Designed by Kamae Design
Produced and Typeset by Sparks, Oxford – www.sparks.co.uk
Printed in China (SWTC/04)
Cover photo/illustration © Steve Shott

Acknowledgements
Microsoft product screenshots reprinted with permission from Microsoft Corporation.

Every effort has been made to contact copyright holders of material reproduced in this book. Any omissions will be rectified in subsequent printings if notice is given to the publishers.

Websites
The websites used in this book were correct and up-to-date at the time of publication. It is essential for tutors to preview each website before using it in class so as to ensure that the URL is still accurate, relevant and appropriate. We suggest that tutors bookmark useful websites and consider enabling students to access them through the school/college intranet.

Ordering Information
Payne-Gallway, FREEPOST (OF1771),
PO Box 381, Oxford OX2 8BR
Tel: 01865 888070
Fax: 01865 314029
Email: orders@payne-gallway.co.uk

Contents

Series Introduction

Introduction

This book is one of a series of books that has been designed to guide you in your work for the OCR Level 2 Nationals in ICT. Each book covers two or three units and explains the skills and concepts that are needed for each. It also sets out in detail how to create a portfolio to achieve a Pass, **Merit** or Distinction for each Assessment Objective.

Webpage Creation and *Creating Animation for the WWW Using ICT* covers the Assessment Objectives (AOs) as set out in Units 2 and 20 of the specification. In addition, there is an introductory practice assignment for Units 2 and 20 which helps you to assess how well you can create, test and evaluate a website in response to a brief from a client.

> **To access the practice assignments, go to Units 2 and 20 under *Student Resources* on the www.payne-gallway.co.uk website**

How to use this book

The book is divided into two sections which guide you through each Assessment Objective (AO) as set out by OCR for Units 2 and 20. Every chapter helps you to understand how you would build evidence for your portfolio through clearly identified Scenarios, helpful Tips and structured Activities using step-by-step instructions. At every stage clear guidance is given as to the level of evidence required for a Pass, **Merit** or Distinction so that you are able to plan your own progress effectively.

Each student book in the series is further supported by data files for use with some of the activities. These are available for download at the Payne-Gallway website www.payne-gallway.co.uk.

UNIT ②

Webpage Creation

In this unit you will cover the following...

→ **A01** Plan a website of at least five pages using a range of techniques

→ **A02** Create and use either a template or cascading style sheets to create your web pages, adding text, images and a variety of other media, including sound

→ **A03** Create simple textual hyperlinks and develop this skill further by creating buttons, hotspots, menus and navigation bars

→ **A04** Add interactivity to your website

→ **A05** Create a form which includes a submit button and elements such as drop-down boxes in order to collect feedback from users of your website

→ **A06** Carry out testing and understand *why* you need to test your website

→ **A07** Evaluate your work and create your own design table to organise your testing

Introduction to Unit 2
The Practice Assignment: Sam's Website

Unit 2 assesses how well you can create, test and evaluate a website in response to a brief from a client. So that you can do this, you will learn how to produce a website using Dreamweaver.

In order to practise and consolidate the skills you will acquire in this unit, you will apply them to a practice assignment: *Sam's website*.

Your friend, Sam, has asked you to create a five-page website for her band. She has asked you to include web pages on the following topics:

→ band members

→ contact details

→ a page for fans to give feedback about gigs

→ a page showing future gigs.

You have also suggested that the website should have a homepage, which will introduce visitors to the site and give basic information about the band.

At the end of Unit 2, you will submit a website in response to a brief. It should be noted that this website must be *your own work*. The website you produce for the practice assignment (Sam's website) must not be submitted for final assessment.

CHAPTER

→ *Assessment Objective 1*

Design a Multimedia Website

Overview:

In this chapter, you will learn what a multimedia website is. You will then learn how a range of different considerations must be taken into account before you design a website. Once you have learnt these skills, you will explore the different navigation structures you could use for a website and how each of these could be used.

You will then be shown how to design a website so that it takes account of all of these features. At the end of the chapter, you will be introduced to the plan for the website you will produce for Sam.

How this assessment objective will be assessed...

- Your work for Assessment Objective 1 must be in the form of a proposal for a website. This proposal should include a discussion of how well the website will meet its purpose and the needs of the target audience.
- You must also include a site plan for your website as well as a plan for each web page.
- The overall quality of your work will be assessed by how much detail you include in your proposal and design.

Skills to use...

- You will need to show that you can measure the needs of a target audience for your website and plan a product which uses a range of web elements to meet those needs.
- Your plans must be accurate. This means that well-drawn and well-laid-out plans which make sense to the viewer are more likely to score highly than poorly presented rough sketches.
- Your work must show that you can design a website of at least five pages which will be navigable.

How to achieve...

Pass requirements

P1 You will produce a brief proposal for a website of at least five pages. The proposal will include some details about the purpose of the website and the target audience.

P2 You will produce a site plan for your website. This plan will show a basic house style and simple page plans for five pages as well as links between the pages.

P3 The page plans produced may contain some errors.

Merit requirements

M1 You will produce a detailed proposal for a website of at least five pages. The proposal will include clear details about both the purpose of the website and the target audience.

M2 You will produce a site plan for your website. This plan will show a suitable house style and accurate detailed plans for five pages.

M3 The site plan will show more than one possible way to link the pages together.

Distinction requirements

D1 You will produce a comprehensive proposal for a website of at least five pages. The proposal will include clear details about both the purpose of the website and the target audience.

D2 You will produce a detailed site plan for your website. This plan will show a detailed house style, with detailed plans for at least five pages, clearly showing links.

D3 The site plan will include clear planning of colour scheme and the inclusion of multimedia elements.

Designing a multimedia website

Your completed work for this unit will be presented as a portfolio. This portfolio will include evidence to show that you have created a working, navigable multimedia website which you have both planned and tested.

You must start by producing a detailed plan for your multimedia website. The OCR specifications for this unit state that this should be a **proposal** for a website.

Key terms

Proposal

A document which explains the structure, design and intended audience for a website.

What is a multimedia website?

We need to deal with this question before we go any further with this chapter. Simply put, a multimedia website is a website which includes multimedia elements. There are five main **elements** that may be combined to make up a multimedia website:

* graphics
* animation
* sound
* text
* video.

The website you design and produce should combine a range of these elements.

Writing the proposal

Your proposal should include the following:

1 the purpose of the website
2 the target audience for the website
3 a site plan for the website
4 an indication of house style
5 plans for each page, showing elements on the page and any hyperlinks.

We will discuss each of these issues in turn. We will start with the purpose of the website.

The purpose of the website

When you come to complete your work for this unit, you will need to decide on the **purpose** of your website – what the website is trying to do. Websites are created for many different reasons. Below is a short list of reasons why a website may be created:

- to inform
- to generate sales
- to increase sales
- to publicise
- to share information between people.

You will probably be able to think of many other reasons why websites are created.

If the website you are producing is based on a **brief** given by your centre, it should be clear what the purpose of the website is from the instructions you are given. If the purpose is not clear, it is likely that your teacher will be acting as a client. This means that while there is no real customer for whom you are working, your teacher will pretend to be the customer and will answer any queries you have. If you are working on your own choice of brief, make sure that you are clear about the purpose before you start.

Key terms

Purpose

What a website is trying to do.

Brief

The instructions given for a task.

How does this apply to Sam's website?

The purpose of your friend Sam's website is to publicise her band and to get more gigs. The audiences for the band are generally aged between 16 and 30 and are an equal split between females and males. The band play a mixture of pop and rock music and want to appeal to people who like that sort of music. Therefore, they want a website which suits this image.

Target audience

Target audience is a very important concept, as it is the group of people at whom a product is aimed. For a general product, such as a type of food eaten by a wide range of people, there would be a very large target audience. An example of such a product may be burgers sold in a chain of restaurants. Many different types of people will eat such food and so the advertising and publicity for this product need to be quite general. However, for other products, such as specialist books, there will be a very narrow target audience, as only people who are interested in the subject matter for these books would buy them. An example of this would be a book of locomotive numbers published for train-spotters. Any train-spotters reading this book will now be protesting that this is not a narrow interest and there are thousands of people who share the hobby. However, even the keenest train-spotter will accept that there are more people who eat burgers than spot trains and so will accept that the book itself, as well as any advertising, must appeal to that relatively narrow target audience.

Target audiences are usually defined by the characteristics of the group that a product is aimed at. There are many ways to describe a target audience and some are listed below:

- **geography** – a local newsletter, for example, will appeal to a small group of people who live in a certain area
- **age** – some products are aimed at people of a certain age. Teenage magazines are a good example of this
- **gender** – products may be aimed at females, at males or at both genders
- **income** – this can be a very influential factor on who buys a product. This is not only a question of the cost of a product but also what the product says about the wealth and income of the people who buy it
- **educational background** – a person's level of education can influence how and what they buy. This is not always as clear-cut as, say, the geographical factor, but can still be influential.

These are just some examples of the different groupings which can be applied to target audiences. These groupings can be combined. For example, the target audience for a regional magazine may be described as 'women over the age of 30 who live in Wales'. If other groups of people choose to read the magazine, this is not important. The target audience is who the product is aimed at and not necessarily who actually uses the product.

Key terms

Target audience

The audience for which a product has been produced.

Activity 1: Target audiences...

In this activity you will:

● use your knowledge and understanding to identify the target audience for a range of products.

For each of the products below, decide who the target audience is:

▶ 50 cc mopeds

▶ baked beans

▶ baby food

▶ CDs of a band famous in the 1990s but who are no longer recording

▶ business suits

▶ football shirts

▶ broadsheet newspapers

▶ tabloid newspapers

▶ broadband Internet access

▶ PDAs.

How does this apply to Sam's website?

It should be clear that the target audience for the website you are creating is:

● aged between 16 and 30
● interested in pop and rock music
● both female and male.

Producing a site plan

Your site plan is the structure of the website, which is basically the order in which each page of the website is linked to the others. There are three possible structures for your website. The first is linear, where the pages are linked one after the other. An example is shown below.

Figure 1.1: *A linear website structure.*

The second option is a hierarchical structure, where web pages are linked into logical sections. An example of this is shown in Figure 1.2.

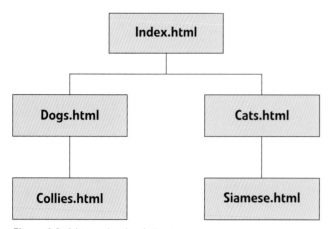

Figure 1.2: *A hierarchical website structure.*

You could use a hierarchical structure if you were designing a website for a school, for example. This would then allow you to have one main web page for each department or faculty, with other web pages leading off this main page giving more information about the department or faculty (e.g. showing subjects taught or information about teachers).

The final possible structure is a mesh structure. In this structure, each page is linked to all the others and the user of the website is able to choose their own path through the website. An example of this structure is shown below.

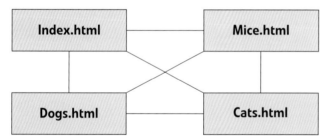

Figure 1.3: *A mesh website structure.*

How does this apply to Sam's website?

The website you are planning for Sam will follow a mesh structure, with each page accessible from each other page. The site plan for this website is shown below.

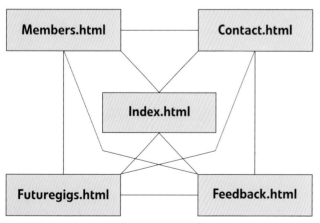

Figure 1.4: *The site plan for Sam's website.*

House style

When you come to complete your own work for this unit, you will need to decide what your completed document will look like. This decision will not only include the structure and use of images, but will also cover other questions about the style of the document. Some of the issues which have a bearing on the style of a document include:

- what type, size and colour of font to use for any text on the page
- whether and how to use justification for any text
- the style of bullets or numbers on the page
- where the logo or business name will appear on the page and whether this is on every page.

When planning, it is always best to set up a table before you start. This means that you are more likely to answer all of the necessary questions. Each of the bullets above has a set of questions which you need to answer. Below are the tables you could use for deciding on how text and images will be used on your website.

	Where used?	Style	Size	Colour
Font				

	Black and white or colour?	Style of image	Size on the page
Images			

How does this apply to Sam's website?

The tables below show the information you have gained from Sam about how text and images will be used on her website. In some cases she knows exactly what she wants but in others she has given you as much information as she can and is asking you to give suggestions.

	Where used	Style	Size	Colour
Font	Main body text	Something quite traditional and old-looking	Size 14 at least	Black

	Black and white or colour?	Style of image	Size on the page
Images	Black and white for posed photos. Colour for shots from gigs.	Posed photos should be quite serious, but live shots should be chosen for what they show about the atmosphere in a gig.	Use one main picture for each page, with at least two other, smaller pictures to break up text.

⊕TIP

You could use similar tables to collect details about how any text and images will be used on your website. Before you visit your client to get design details, create a table like this in a word-processing package for each aspect of design and make sure you ask your client enough questions to complete the tables. Once completed, these tables will then be evidence of how you have designed your website.

Planning a web page

The final stage is to plan each web page. If you want to score highly for Assessment Objective 1, you must create quite detailed plans. A detailed plan is one which makes it very clear what the finished product will look like. When you are planning a web page, ask yourself whether or not someone else could use your plan to create exactly the web page you can see in your mind.

How does this apply to Sam's website?

The detailed plan for the five pages of Sam's website is shown below.

Full-size versions of these scans are also available in the Unit 2 Resources zip file which can be downloaded from the Payne-Gallway website: www.payne-gallway.co.uk.

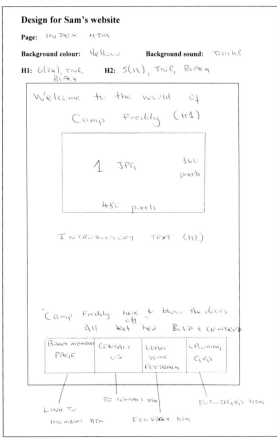

Figure 1.5: Homepage.

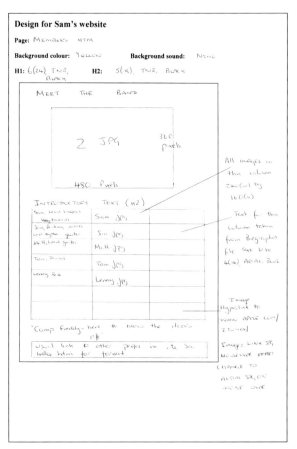

Figure 1.6: Band members.

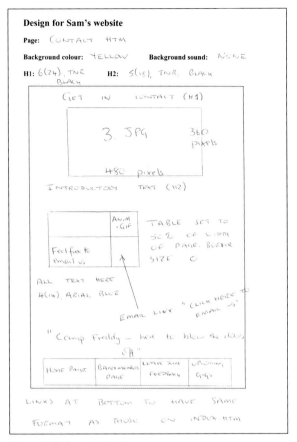

Figure 1.7: *Contact details.*

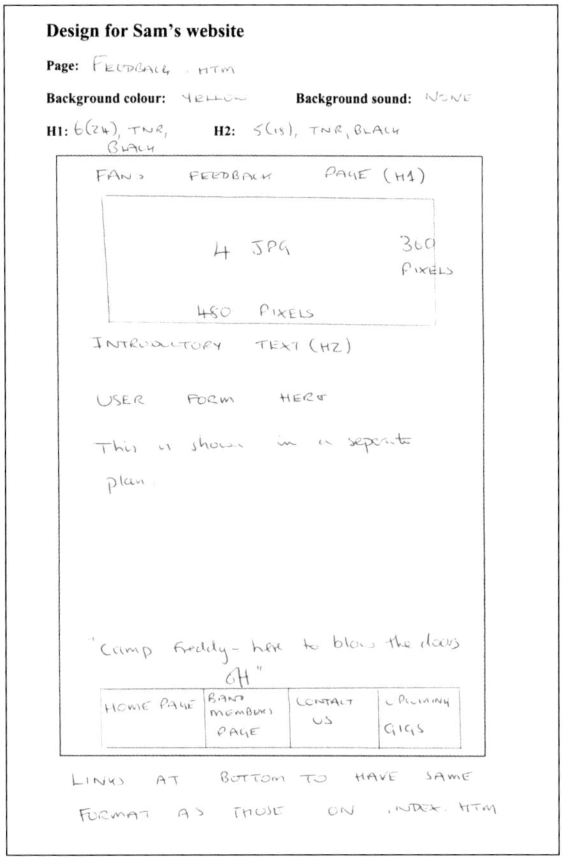

Figure 1.8: *Fans' feedback page.*

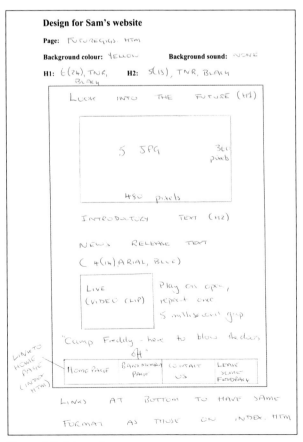

Figure 1.9: *Future gigs.*

There are a few things to remember when planning a web page:

- You do not have to be a great artist! If you cannot draw a tree, put a box where the picture of a tree would go on the finished web page and insert the text '**picture of tree to go here**'.
- If you want to include text, you do not have to type it all in, but you would need to give some indication about what the text will be and also the style of writing you will use.

⊕ TIP

When you plan text, you do not have to include all of it, but you do need to give a bit more detail than 'text to go here'. You should describe what the text will be about. You should also give some indication of how long the piece of writing will be (maybe by saying how many words you will use), as well as describing all the details about font style, size and colour.

- Remember that just because your software sets things up with certain defaults, you cannot assume this is the same for everyone. For example, if you are used to white being set as a background colour, you may forget to include it in your design. However, someone else looking at your design may have different default settings and may choose to use a different setting for background colours. A simple rule of thumb here is to explain everything and not to leave anything to chance.
- Show hyperlinks! This may seem obvious, but it is often forgotten. Your design should show the type of hyperlink you will use, as well as the target of the hyperlink. If you are going to use a graphic hyperlink, you will need to include details about the graphic you will use, as well as all other details.
- Show multimedia components. These would include any animations, video or sound you have chosen to include in your web page. Give some indication about what each multimedia component is.

⊕ TIP

Assessment Objective 5 requires you to include a user form in your completed website. We will look at how to create this later on, but you will need to show a user form in the design you create at this stage. You should spend some time researching user forms on the Internet (and find a design you wish to copy) or jump ahead to Chapter 5 for some hints.

Once you have completed your design, you can start collecting any materials you want to include.

CHAPTER 2

→ Assessment Objective 2

Create Multimedia Web Pages

Overview:

In Part A of this chapter, you will be shown a range of skills and theories which you must understand before you begin to create your website.

The website you create should adhere to a chosen house style, which will be reflected in design decisions such as your choice of text and colour. You should use templates which you create yourself or cascading style sheets to achieve this. These skills, as well as the theory and practice behind creating backups, will all be dealt with in the first part of this chapter.

In Part B, you will be shown how to create the multimedia website you designed for Assessment Objective 1. Your design should show the use of a range of different elements which may be combined to create the finished product. Before you begin to create your website, you will need to gather at least some of these elements. So that your website operates as efficiently as possible, and to aid the process of creating it, you will need to set up a suitable directory structure into which you will be placing these elements.

You should be aware of the following:

* those of you aiming at a **Distinction** grade should use cascading style sheets instead of a template to create a house style for your website
* those aiming at a **Merit** grade should use a cascading style sheet *or* a template
* **Pass** candidates may use only a template.

These two methods of creating a web page are very different and so we will concentrate on the use of templates to create a constant house style as this will also include instructions on how to add elements to your web pages. Once we have covered all of these skills, we will discuss how you might use cascading style sheets to create a house style. **Distinction** candidates should note that they are advised to work through the sections on using templates too, as many important design techniques and ideas are discussed. (See also the note on page 57.)

In order to complete the activities in this chapter you will need access to a number of additional files. These files are contained in the Unit 2 Resources zip file which can be downloaded from the OCR Nationals in ICT (Units 2 & 20) Student Resources page on the Payne-Gallway website: www.payne-gallway.co.uk.

How this assessment objective will be assessed...

When you come to create your website, you will be assessed on the following aspects:

- the directory structure you use to organise the elements used in your website
- the quality of your completed website
- the methods you use to create your website
- the range and quality of suitable images you choose to include in your website
- the use of navigation tools to move around your completed website
- the quality of the printout of your web pages
- the backup procedures you adopt to ensure that your work is not lost.

Skills to use...

- You will need to produce a web page which has a minimum of errors, so make sure that you are proof-reading your work at all times.
- You will need to choose images for inclusion in the website you create. These images must be suitable, so you must keep a clear sense of audience and purpose for your website.
- By the end of this chapter, you will have produced the majority of your website but will still have a few small items to add. You will also have a sensible and usable backup regime in place. Be sure that you understand and are able to use backup techniques and folder structures before you begin producing your web pages.

How to achieve...

Pass requirements

P1 You will create a basic template combining text and a minimum of five different images and use it to produce a simple website.

P2 There may be errors in your work, but the meaning of any work is clear.

P3 Any images you use must be suitable for the purpose.

P4 The website produced must be navigable.

P5 The evidence provided for the website will be printed from the web-browsing software used by you, but some of the content may be missing.

P6 You will provide a screenshot showing a basic directory structure. The directory and filenames used by you may not always be suitable. There may not be evidence of any form of backup.

Merit requirements

M1 You will use either a template you have created or a cascading style sheet to create a website which includes web pages with appropriate styles for headings and body text.

M2 There may be some errors in your work, but the meaning of the work is clear.

M3 There will be some use of tables in the website.

M4 There will be a range of suitable images used in the website. These images will be of good quality and scaled in proportion. There will be evidence in the form of screen-shots to prove that some images have been optimised for use on the website.

M5 The website produced must be navigable.

M6 The completed website will have been printed from the web-browsing software used by you.

M7 You will provide a screenshot showing a sound directory structure, with accurate use made of directory and filenames. There will be some evidence in the form of screen-shots that backup procedures are in place.

Distinction requirements

D1 You will use cascading style sheets to produce high-quality web pages.

D2 The meaning of the website will be clear with very few spelling errors.

D3 You will have used tables throughout the website to aid with the layout of different elements.

D4 There will be a good range of suitable images used in the website. These images will be of excellent quality and scaled in proportion. There will be evidence in the form of screenshots to prove that all images have been optimised for use on the website.

D5 The website produced must be navigable.

D6 The completed website will have been printed from the web-browsing software used by you, with whole pages displayed.

D7 You will provide a screenshot showing a good directory structure, with accurate and descriptive use made of directory and filenames. There will be evidence in the form of screenshots that full backup procedures are in place.

Part A

The skills and theory behind creating a website

This chapter will start by looking at the background skills and theory you will need to understand in order to create a website. We will look at the following:

1 directory structures
2 filenames
3 backups
4 working with house styles
5 creating templates
6 creating cascading style sheets.

Directory structure

You will need to create a logical directory structure which lets you store elements of your website so that they are easy to find. One possible way of doing this is to organise the resources so that all images are in the same directory, with all other resources in one massive directory. This is quite a simple structure and probably not the best.

An alternative would be to place all images in one directory, with all other shared resources (such as sound or video files) in a directory called **shared resources**. This would then allow you to organise your resources more easily. If you have a lot of resources to go into each of the five pages, but which are not used elsewhere, you could set up a directory for each page of your website.

You should also choose descriptive and accurate names for your directories. Directory names such as **stuff** or **website bits** are not at all helpful. Try to name your directory so that you are never unsure where to place an element and anyone looking at your structure would be able to understand it immediately. Directory names such as **shared images** or **shared videos** are far more descriptive and will make your work easier.

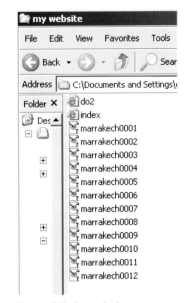

Figure 2.1: *A simple directory structure.*

How does this apply to Sam's website?

You have already seen the plan for Sam's website. So that you can organise your resources, you are going to use a folder structure which allows you to save all images in one directory. As with all other skills you learn in this chapter, you will use this one later when you come to create Sam's website.

Figure 2.2: *A more logical directory structure.*

Filenames

Below is a list of files that have been used in a website about fish.

- new_page_1.htm
- new_page_2.htm
- new_page_3.htm
- new_page_4.htm

These filenames are not very clear. The list below shows the same website, but this time more descriptive filenames have been used.

- index.htm
- aquarium.htm
- seafish.htm
- freshwater.htm

TIP

Remember to use appropriate names for files as well as directories!

If you look at the two file lists, you should see the benefit of having filenames which are clear and easy to understand. You may be convinced that you would be able to remember the contents of each page in the first list, but imagine what would happen if your website grew into twenty pages or even more. By using descriptive names for each page of your website, you will be saving yourself a good deal of time and worry later on. It is a good habit to get into, even with relatively small websites, and is also something which is stressed as one of the criteria for Assessment Objective 2.

How does this apply to Sam's website?

The use of descriptive filenames is a good habit to get into and, as you shall see later, it is one that will be used in the creation of Sam's website.

Keeping backups

Computers, like any other machines, do sometimes fail. To avoid the risk of losing your work, you will need to make backups. If you are producing your website at your school or college, you will find that there is a policy about backups. This will probably involve a daily network backup. However, the instructions for this course make it clear that you must set up your own backup procedure. As a basic idea, you should ensure that every time you make a change to your website, you make an electronic copy of your website on a medium or device which can be taken away with you. The choice of device or medium to which you save, such as CD, USB memory stick or external hard drive may be governed by school policy – some schools ban USB hard drives, for example. Whichever device or medium you choose, save your work after each session.

If you are producing work at home or elsewhere, do not fool yourself into thinking that your machine will not fail. Just as if you were working at school or college, you must save a copy of your work after each session.

You will need to provide screenshot evidence of having a working backup system in place. There are a number of ways in which you could do this but a screenshot of the directory structure showing a removable drive and the day-by-day content of that drive as you change your website is one possible method. Another method involves producing a screen-shot of a CD being created as data is moved across.

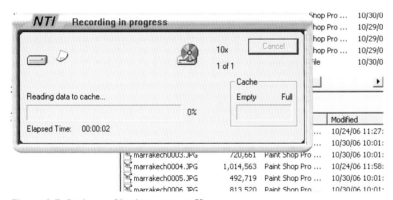

Figure 2.3: *Evidence of backing up on a CD.*

Working with house styles

Before you create your web pages, you need to give some thought to the issue of **house style** which we discussed in the first chapter. As you will remember, the house style is basically rules for how elements look on each page. There are three main ways of setting a house style across your website.

1 Create each page one by one and make sure all the headings and other elements suit the rules of your house style. This is not the best method and can take a lot of time and organisation to do. Because of the large amount of work required, you are quite likely to make mistakes if you follow this method! This method is the most basic and does not get rewarded within the mark scheme for this unit.

2 Create a template of your own to suit the house style for the website. This will set basic designs for elements such as:

- the background
- text styles and colours
- hyperlink styles and colours
- general features such as banners
- choices about navigation.

If you follow this method, your work for Assessment Objective 2 is likely to be either in the Pass or **Merit** mark band.

3 Use a cascading style sheet. This is the most impressive method and will earn you most respect from the OCR Visiting Moderator (VM) if you do it correctly. It is too complicated to explain in a few sentences, so we will come back to it later in this chapter. In the meantime, we will look at how you create a template.

> ⊙TIP
>
> Remember to look back at the marking grid for this unit. If you are targeting a Pass grade for this unit, you can create the web pages using a basic template you have created. If you are targeting a Merit pass, you should use either a more complex template or cascading style sheets. If you are targeting a Distinction, you cannot use a template and must use a cascading style sheet to set the styles within your web pages.

Dreamweaver sites

Key terms

HTML code

The language for describing the structure of a web page. Web pages can be created by writing this code directly.

Web authoring software

WYSIWYG ('what you see is what you get') software used to create web pages without the need for the user to understand or be able to write HTML code.

All of the examples given on creating the website will be from Dreamweaver. This is **web authoring** software which allows you to set how a page will look on screen, just as if you were creating a desktop-publishing document. However, you can also check the **HTML** code behind the web page simply by clicking on the **Code** button at the top of the page. Do not worry if you do not have this software, as most website authoring packages will have the same sort of layout and include the same sort of tools and facilities. What follows is an explanation of creating templates when using Dreamweaver.

First of all you need to open Dreamweaver. This can be done by:

- *either* clicking on the icon (if there is one) on your desktop
- *or* clicking on **Start, All Programs, Macromedia, Macromedia Dreamweaver 8**.

If your computer is set up slightly differently, check with your teacher. Some schools and colleges may choose to use a folder called **core** to store links to standard software packages. Others may put all software related to creating websites into a folder called something like **web creation software**.

Once the software has opened, your screen should look like the screenshot below.

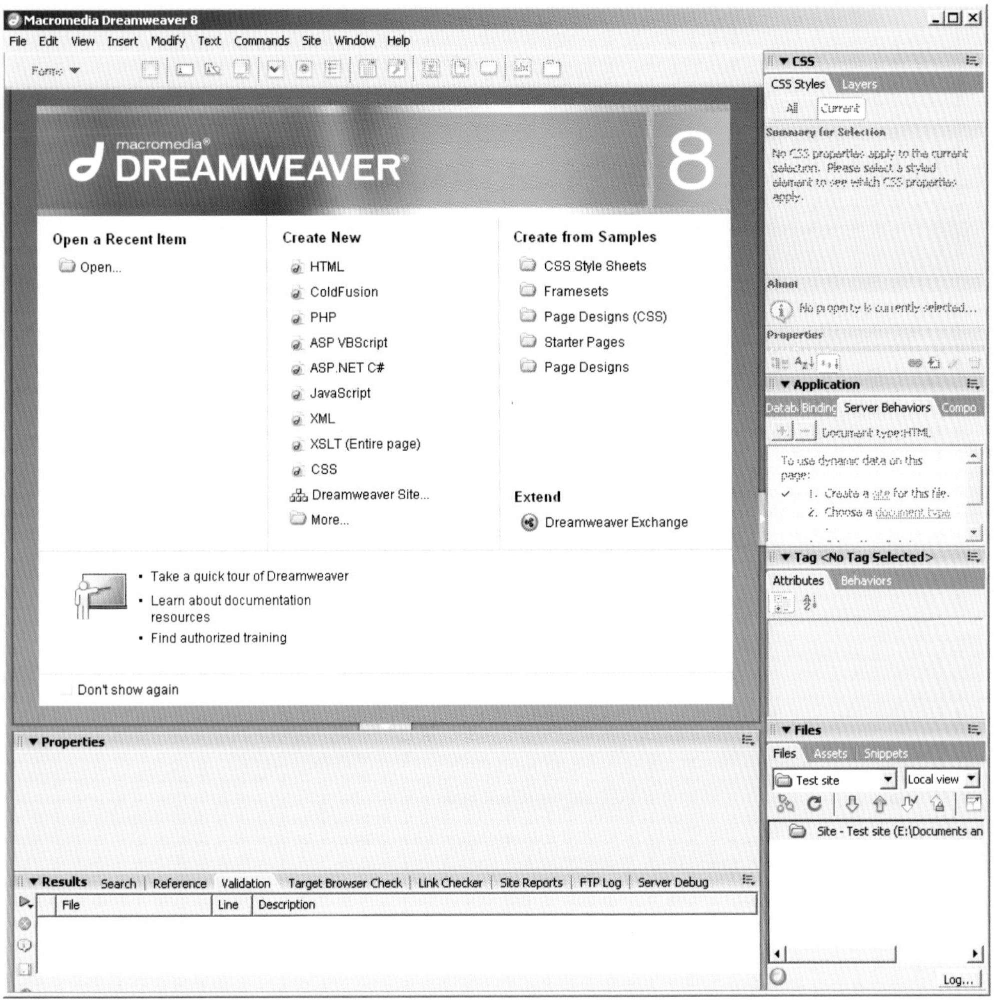

Figure 2.4: *The opening page for Macromedia Dreamweaver.*

Before you create any web pages, you must create a work area on disk. In Dreamweaver these work areas are called **sites**. Your first task is to set up a site to hold the files and settings for the website that you will create for this unit.

Activity 1: Creating a Dreamweaver site...

In this activity you will:

● create a site to hold the files and settings for a website.

▶ Use the **Site...New Site** menu to open the **Site Definition** dialogue box.

▶ Type in a unique name for your website. You would usually use a name that describes the content of the site, but for this example you can use your own name or any other name that nobody else will be using.

▶ You don't need a URL, so just click **Next**.

▶ You won't be using server technology (e.g. creating web pages dynamically from the contents of a database), so click **Next** again.

▶ Check with your teacher where you should save the site, and make sure that the path matches, then click **Next**.

▶ Select **None** from the drop-down list, then click **Next**.

▶ A summary page will appear. Click **Done** to create the new site.

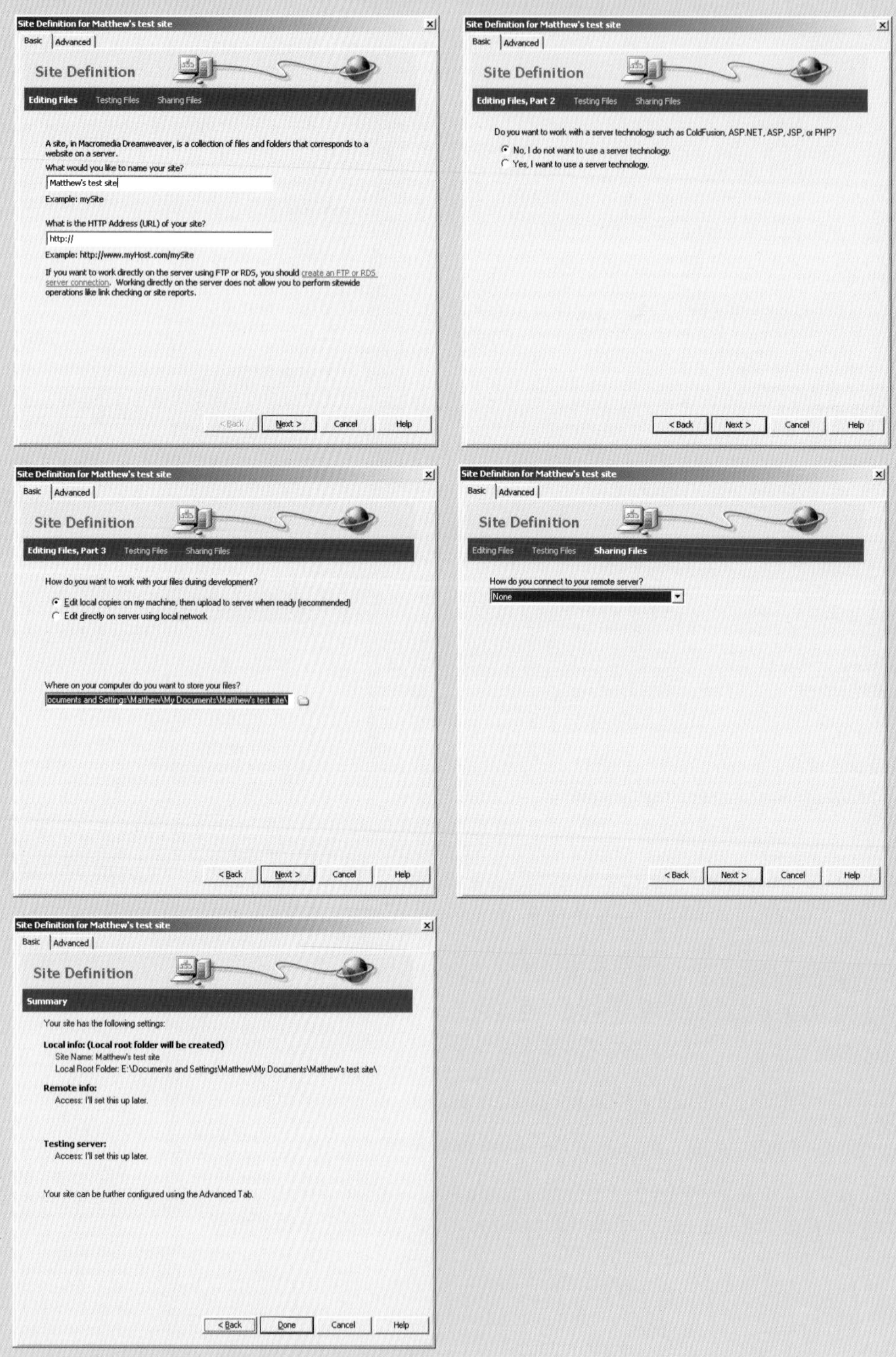

Figure 2.5: *The steps needed to create a simple site.*

Creating templates

In the activity below, you will work through a practice assignment to create a simple template. To do so, you will need to be able to add a heading to a page and to choose the font type and size. These are both chosen from drop-down lists.

Imagine you have been asked to construct a website by your teacher. You have been given the following design specifications for the website you must create. To help you, you decide to create a template to use when working.

The design specifications are shown in the table below.

Web page element	Style
Heading for each page	Courier font, size 24, centred on each page
Introductory text	Arial, left-aligned, font size 12
Main body text	Times New Roman, left aligned, font size 12, colour – blue
Background	Colour – yellow
Hyperlinks	Unvisited – lime
	Visited – purple

Activity 2: Creating a template...

In this activity you will:

- create a simple template (this is for practice purposes only).

   ▶ Use **File...New** to display the **New from Template** dialogue box.

   ▶ Click the **General** tab and then select **Template page** and **HTML template**, as shown below. Click **Create**.

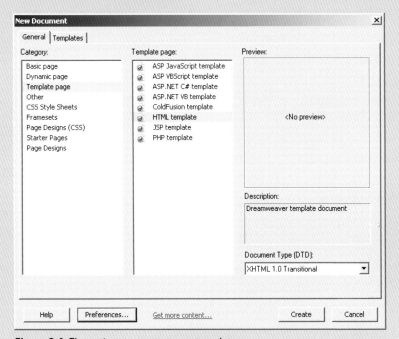

Figure 2.6: *The options to create a new template.*

A web page template is simply a page that has been set up with all of the basic bits already done for you; it also gives you clues about where to add elements later. All you have to do is to overwrite the bits that give you clues. Dreamweaver allows you to specify which areas of the template will be editable in the pages created from the template – this prevents things from being accidentally deleted, and means that the template can easily be updated and the changes applied to all of the pages based on the template.

▶ At the top of the blank page you have just created, type **Heading 1**. Select this section and choose the following using the **Properties** panel:
  - **Courier New, Courier, monospace** font (notice how several alternative font names are given so that the page will look similar on various types of computer)
  - font size **24**
  - centred on the page (click the **Align Center** icon).

  This is where you will add the heading for each page when you come to create your web pages later in this chapter.

▶ Click in the white space below the heading and press **Enter** twice to come down two lines.

▶ Change the font style to **Arial, Helvetica, sans serif**, size **12**. Type **Introductory text**.

▶ You will now use the background options to choose a few more style settings for your web page template. Use the **Modify...Page Properties** menu to display the **Page Properties** dialogue box. This is a great interface form because, not only can you choose a background image or colour, but you can also set things like the default font colour and how textual hyperlinks will appear. The design specifications for this website show that the background of this template should be **yellow** and the default text colour **blue**. Unvisited hyperlinks should be **lime**, with visited ones **purple**. Make the appropriate changes and click **OK**.

▶ Below this text, add a horizontal line using **Insert...HTML...Horizontal Rule**.

▶ Below the line, type **Copyright notice goes here**.

  Now you need to specify which parts of the template will be editable in web pages based on the template. Any areas not marked as editable will be fixed, and it will only be possible to change them by editing the template itself.

▶ Select the text **Heading 1** and then select **Insert...Template Objects...Editable Region**. Type **Main Heading** in the **New Editable Region** dialogue box and then click **OK**.

▶ Repeat this process to change **Introductory text** into an editable region called **Body Text**.

▶ You have now finished choosing all of the settings for your template. Click **File... Save**. If you see a warning that your editable region is inside a block tag, just press **OK**. You will learn how to fix this problem in Activity 19 (page 43)

▶ The **Save As Template** dialogue box should appear. Type **Testing Template** as the name, and add a suitable description.

(►) Click **Save** to finish the process of creating your own template. The template will be saved as a .dwt file, and will appear in your list of templates when you come to create a new file.

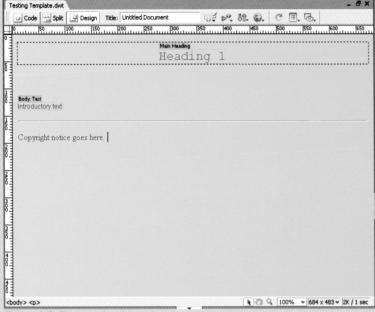

Figure 2.7: *The completed template.*

Activity 3: Creating a simple web page from a template...

In this activity you will:

● create a simple web page based on the template you created.

(►) Use **File...New** from the menu to display the dialogue box that lets you create a new page.

(►) With the **Templates** tab selected, click on the name of the template you created earlier.

(►) Click the **Create** button to create a new web page based on the template.

Notice that you can only edit those parts of the page that you specified as editable in the template.

(►) Change the heading and body text, just to prove that you can.

(►) Save the page as **Based on template.html**.

▶ Edit **Testing Template.dwt**, changing the copyright line to read **Copyright [*your name*] [*year*]**.

▶ Save the template, and update the files based on the template when prompted to do so.

▶ Open **Based on template.html** and check that its copyright line has been updated to match the template. You can imagine how useful this would be if you had a very large website – you could change the copyright line in one place, instead of having to edit each page in turn.

Cascading style sheets

If you are targeting a **Distinction** grade, you must use a cascading style sheet to ensure that your web pages all follow the same rules. Cascading style sheets are like templates, in that they set up how elements will look on the web page. However, unlike templates, they work directly with **HTML**, the code behind web pages, to change the settings for elements on any page which uses the cascading style sheet. They are used for two purposes:

● So that elements on web pages will look as much like the author required, irrespective of which **browser** is being used.
● To reduce the amount of code used to create web pages. You may think that this is irrelevant because you are using web page authoring software, rather than HTML code, to create your website. However, if you can reduce the amount of code used to create your website, you will also reduce the time it takes for your website to open.

There are three different types of cascading style sheet:

1 External – an external cascading style sheet keeps the rules in a separate file. This means that you can apply the cascading style sheet rules to all pages in the website.
2 Embedded – an embedded cascading style sheet is held in one page and can only apply to that page. If you were using an external cascading style sheet to define all of the settings on your website, but wanted one page to be slightly different, you could use an embedded cascading style sheet on that page only, which would let you make your design changes.
3 Inline – an inline cascading style sheet is used to set style settings for one element on a web page.

You can see that the difference between these three types is how much of your website they affect. We will concentrate on the use of external cascading style sheets, as these are more than enough for this qualification.

Creating cascading style sheets

Dreamweaver includes a range of styles, but as you are expected to create templates for the **Pass** and **Merit** levels, it seems logical that you would want to create a cascading style sheet of your own. The easiest way of doing this is to use HTML. A further advantage of using HTML is that you will be able to employ this technique which- ever web authoring package you use.

Figure 2.8: *The Code, Split and Design tabs.*

Dreamweaver, like many other web page authoring packages, allows you to see your web page either in **Design** view, which is the view in which you have been working up to now, or in **Code** view, which is the code behind your web page. There is also a **Split** view that shows the design and the code together. You can edit your web page in any view.

Activity 4: Creating a cascading style sheet...

In this activity you will:

● create a cascading style sheet which defines background colour, Heading 1 and Heading 2.

▶ Open Dreamweaver and use **File...New** from the menu. With the **General** tab selected, click **CSS Style Sheets** and **Basic: Arial**. Click **Create**.

This creates a simple cascading style sheet that formats elements using the Arial font, as follows:

```
body {
        font-family: Arial, Helvetica, sans-serif;
}

td {
        font-family: Arial, Helvetica, sans-serif;
}

th {
        font-family: Arial, Helvetica, sans-serif;
}
```

There are two ways to modify the style sheet's properties: by using the drop-down menus in the **CSS** pane or by editing the text. You can try both methods.

▶ Click anywhere in the **body{ }** element in the text of the CSS page.

▶ Click the **Add Property** link in the **CSS** pane. Select **background-color** from the first drop-down list, then click the coloured square and choose red, as shown in Figure 2.9.

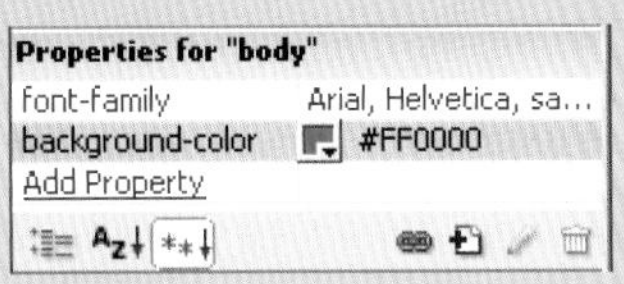

Figure 2.9: *Changing CSS properties.*

Notice that the CSS text is automatically updated to include a new line:

```
        background-color: #FF0000;
```

Now, edit the rest of the CSS text so that it is as follows (notice that you must change the element names to **h1** and **h2**):

```
body {
        font-family: Arial, Helvetica, sans-serif;
        background-color: #FF0000;
}

h1 {
        font-family: Arial, Helvetica, sans-serif;
        font-size: x-large;
        color: blue;
}
```

```
h2 {
        font-family: Arial, Helvetica, sans-serif;
        font-size: large;
        color: yellow;
}
```

▶ Save your sheet as **style1.css**. You have now created a cascading style sheet, which has been saved in the general area of your website.

You should note that all instructions must be enclosed by curly brackets {}. It is also important that you use gaps between instructions, and semicolons to show when instructions end.

Once you have created a cascading style sheet, you will need to apply it to any pages you want it to control. Again, this is quite complicated when using web authoring packages but is quite easy when working with HTML.

Before you apply your cascading style sheet, you will need to create a simple web page. The activity below shows you how to do this.

Activity 5: Creating a simple web page...

In this activity you will:

● create a simple web page without any formatting.

▶ Use **File...New** from the menu to display the dialogue box that lets you create a new page.

▶ With the **General** tab selected, choose **Basic Page** and **HTML** from the two lists, and then click **Create**.

▶ Making sure you are in **Design** view, choose the **Heading 1** setting from the drop-down list in the **Properties** pane and type the following text:

Welcome to my webpage

▶ Come down two lines, choose **Heading 2** and type the text:

A day in the life of me!

▶ Save this file as **myweb.html**. Your web page should look like the one shown below.

Figure 2.10: *The web page you have created.*

Activity 6: Applying a cascading style sheet...

In this activity you will:

● apply the cascading style sheet to the web page you have just created.

This is a reasonably simple task. You should start by changing to the **Code** view of the web page you have just created. At the top of the page you will see a section which begins <head> and ends </head>.

▶ Place your cursor just before the </head> tag and press **enter**.

▶ In this new space, type **<link rel="stylesheet" href="style1.css" />**.

Your HTML code should now look like this:

<!DOCTYPE html PUBLIC "-//W3C//DTD XHTML 1.0 Transitional//EN" "http://www.w3.org/TR/xhtml1/DTD/xhtml1-transitional.dtd">

<html xmlns="http://www.w3.org/1999/xhtml">

<head>

<meta http-equiv="Content-Type" content="text/html; charset=iso-8859-1" />

<title>Untitled Document</title>

<link rel="stylesheet" href="style1.css" />

</head>

<body>

<h1>Welcome to my webpage</h1>

<p> </p>

<h2>A day in the life of me! </h2>

</body>

</html>

▶ Now save your web page. Choose the **Design** tab and you should see that your web page has now changed.

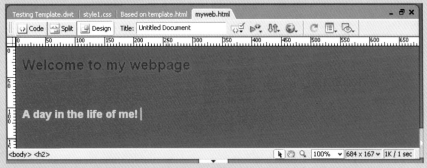

***Figure 2.11:** Your web page with style1.css applied.*

We will do more work with cascading style sheets when we come to work on Sam's website on page 56.

How can I provide evidence I have done this?

Good question! How is anyone going to know whether you have created a template, or just been really organised when you created the web pages? How is anyone going to know if you have created a complex or a simple template, and whether you have used CSS? There are two possible ways to show how you have created your web pages:

1 Witness statements – if a teacher completes a witness statement which explains what you have done and how you did it, this will be an acceptable form of evidence.

2 Screenshots – you could provide screenshots showing that you have created each element and then saved your work as a template. Screenshots are mentioned throughout the specifications for this unit, so it is probably better to use this method to provide evidence of what you have done.

Ideally, you should provide both forms of evidence, as it should leave anyone who is trying to assess your work with no doubt as to how you have completed your work.

If you are working with a cascading style sheet, you should provide a printout of the cascading style sheet's code, as well as a printout of the HTML code used to create any web pages to which the cascading style sheet has been linked. This code will include a reference to the cascading style sheet and so it will be clear that you have used a cascading style sheet in your work.

Part B

Enough of the theory – let's begin!

During Part B of this chapter you will be shown a range of new skills which you will use to create Sam's website. When you come to apply these skills to your own website, you should review what you have learnt here and plan and develop your own website in response to the brief you are set. Do not just copy Sam's website and submit it as your own design.

Creating the folder structure

Before we go on, you will need to create the folder structure you will use for this project.

Activity 7: Creating a folder structure...

In this activity you will:

● work on the structure of Sam's website.

▶ The **Files** pane shows the structure of your website. At present, it looks like Figure 2.12.

You will recall that this is not quite the structure you needed. To make the structure fit the plans, you will need to add four folders.

▶ Right click your site in the **Files** pane and select **New Folder** from the menu that appears. Name the new folder **music**.

Figure 2.12: *Initial folder structure.*

(▶) You should now continue to create and name the remaining three folders:
- **videos**
- **general**
- **images**

Your folder structure should then look like Figure 2.13 (note that the view has been refreshed by clicking the **Refresh** icon ⟳, which changes the order).

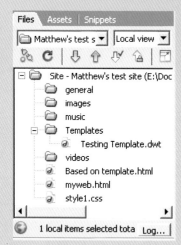

Figure 2.13: *The final folder structure.*

Adding downloaded components

Now you need to move the contents of the **website components** folder into the folders you have just produced. To keep your work organised, all images should be in the **images** folder, the video should be in the **videos** folder and the sound file in the **music** folder.

There are two ways to add resources to the folders in your website: by importing or by copying and pasting. We will concentrate on image files for this exercise, as there are more of those than any other type of element.

Import

If you add an image to a web page, and the image isn't already located in a folder within the site, Dreamweaver offers to create a copy of the file.

Activity 8: Importing files...

In this activity you will:

- learn how to import files into a folder.

(▶) Open **myweb.html**, if it isn't already open.

(▶) Select **Insert...Image** from the menu.

(▶) Navigate to where you have saved the **web resources** folder. Open this folder.

(▶) Select an image and click **OK**.

▶ Dreamweaver asks if you would like to copy the file. Click **Yes**.

Figure 2.14: *The confirmation dialogue box.*

▶ Navigate to the **images** folder in your site and click **Save**.

▶ For now, just click **OK** to dismiss the **Image Tag Accessibility Attributes** dialogue box.

▶ The file you have just selected will now be part of the page, and will appear in the **Files** pane.

Copy and paste

An alternative way to import images is to copy and paste them using Windows Explorer.

Activity 9: Copying and pasting files...

In this activity you will:

● learn how to copy and paste files into a folder.

▶ Open Windows Explorer (the easy way to do this is to hold down the **Start/Windows** key and press **E**).

▶ Navigate to the **web resources** folder and select the images you wish to copy into the **images** folder of your website.

▶ Either choose **Copy** from the **Edit** drop-down menu or use **CTRL+C**.

▶ Navigate to the **images** folder and insert your image, either by choosing **Paste** from the **Edit** drop-down menu, or by using **CTRL+V**.

▶ Use this technique to copy all of your resources to the appropriate folders under your site.

Sam's website design

You are now going to begin to create Sam's website. To do so, you will create a template which follows the specifications from Sam's designs. You should see that there is a very clear design theme running through these pages. This theme is reviewed below.

Each page has the following:

● a heading, which is in **Heading 1** style, which uses font size 6 (24 pt), Times New Roman font and is black

- an image immediately below this heading. This image must be 480 pixels wide and 360 pixels high
- a short piece of text just below this image. This text is **Heading 2** style, which is the same as heading 1, except that the font size is 5(18 pt)
- all other text on the page is Arial, font size 4(14 pt) and blue
- a constant background colour (yellow)
- all unvisited links on the website should be in red and bold and at the bottom of the page.

Creating the template

You are now going to create the template for Sam's website. You will start by creating a blank template and then you will add content as you go along. We will begin by adding all of the text elements. Sam's website will use text of different sizes, font types and colours. You will be shown how to create text which fits Sam's design.

Dreamweaver is a **WYSIWYG** program. This means that adding new text is simply a case of using your mouse to choose where you want to start writing and then using the keyboard to enter text. If this sounds pretty simple, that's probably because it is!

Dreamweaver also has a number of preset styles which can be chosen from the **Format** drop-down list in the **Properties** pane and from the **Text** toolbar.

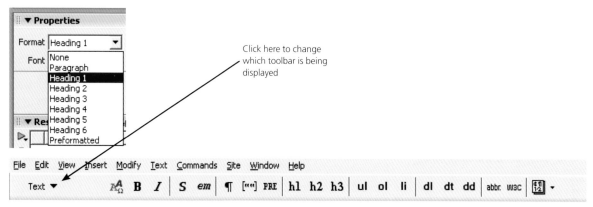

Figure 2.15: *The Format drop-down list and the Text toolbar.*

These properties insert an **HTML tag**. When a web page is viewed in a browser, any settings for tags which are controlled by a cascading style sheet can be applied.

Key terms

WYSIWYG programs

WYSIWYG refers to 'what you see is what you get'. When working with Dreamweaver, this means that if you put a piece of text on a page, Dreamweaver will sort out the HTML code for you. You can therefore play with the design of a page and make quite complex web pages, without any real knowledge of HTML code.

HTML tags

These are the parts of HTML code which identify sections of coding. A tag may be used to show where, for example, the Heading 1 style is to be used.

Activity 10: Creating the template for Sam's website...

In this activity you will:

- create the template for Sam's website
- insert text
- use preset styles.

Make sure that the test site you created is open in Dreamweaver. You will be building Sam's website here.

⏵ Use **File...New** to display the **New Document** dialogue box. Select **Template page** and **HTML Template**, then click **Create**. We will use this page to create the template for Sam's website.

Let's create a title.

⏵ Place your cursor at the top of the page and type **Page heading**. This text will not look very impressive, so we will now change how this text looks by applying a heading style.

⏵ Select the heading you have added and choose **Heading 1** from the **Format** drop-down list or by pressing the **h1** button on the **Text** menu.

⏵ Move down two lines (hit **enter** twice on the keyboard).

⏵ Add the following text in **Heading 2** style:

Introductory text

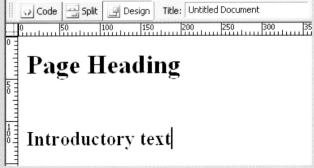

Figure 2.16: *Your template with the main heading and introductory text added.*

Setting attributes and other formats for text

There are a range of different settings you can use with text. These control things such as the following:

- font style
- font size
- text colour
- text alignment
- text attributes (bold, underline and italics).

You have already set some of these when you used the Heading 1 and Heading 2 styles. However, you will sometimes need to set them without using preset styles.

Font style

Dreamweaver includes many different font styles from which you can choose. The current font style for the selected text is shown in the **Properties** pane. (You should note that Figure 2.17 shows the **Properties** pane for **myweb.html** rather than the page you are currently creating. This is because it demonstrates more clearly the fields on display.)

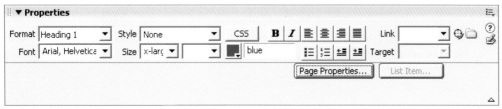

Figure 2.17: *The Properties pane.*

Activity 11: Applying a font style...

In this activity you will:

● apply a chosen font style.

▶ Click on the down arrow to the right of the **Font** label. This will open up a drop-down list of font families from which you can choose.

▶ Choose the set of fonts you want to use from this drop-down list by clicking on your chosen option. (You can use the **Edit Font List** option if you wish to use other fonts that aren't in the list.) The font style you have chosen will now be displayed in the **Properties** pane.

Any text you now add to the page will be in this font style. If you want to add any text in another font, other than in areas which you may have set up using a template, you will need to change your current font style.

If you want to change the font style of a piece of text you have already written, select the text and change the font style as explained above.

How does this apply to Sam's website?

We need to add a section for what is called **body text**. This is basically all of the text on the page apart from headings and hyperlinks. Sam's design shows that this must be in Arial.

▶ Click below where you have added the section in **Heading 2** style and then press **enter**.

▶ The format will change to **Paragraph** in the **Properties** pane.

▶ Choose **Arial, Helvetica, sans-serif** from the drop-down **Font** list.

▶ Add a piece of text saying

    Main body text

Font size

You now need to change the size of the text you have just added.

Font sizes are set in very much the same way as font styles but some explanation is needed before we carry on.

When you set font sizes using Dreamweaver, you will see that you have a choice ranging from **9** to **36** (or you can type a different number) plus some named options. When you select a number from the list, you can then specify the units that this refers to – by default this will be the number of **pixels**, but **points** is probably better in most cases. The named values are as follows (the actual sizes will depend on the web browser being used):

- xx-small
- x-small
- small
- medium
- large
- x-large
- xx-large

There are also two other sizes – **smaller** and **larger** – that will change the size of the text relative to what it would otherwise be based on the other formatting applied to it.

Activity 12: Changing a font size...

In this activity you will:

- follow the instructions below to apply a chosen font size.

▶ Click on the down arrow to the right of the **Size** label. This will open up a drop-down list of sizes from which you can choose.

▶ Choose the font size you want to use from this drop-down list by clicking on your chosen option. The font size you have chosen will now be displayed in the **Properties** pane.

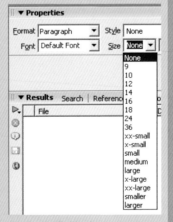

Figure 2.18: *The font size drop-down.*

If you want to change the font size of a piece of text you have already written, select the text and change the font size as explained above.

Note that it is usually better to use CSS to change the sizes of fonts in your web pages, rather than applying the new size in this way.

How does this apply to Sam's website?

▶ Highlight the text you have just added to your template for Sam's website.

▶ From the font size drop-down, choose **14** and change the box next to this to **points**.

Font colour

Colour is another element which can be changed to suit the house style. Before you go on to set the colours for the text on Sam's website, we need to look at the range of colours available in Dreamweaver and how these can be used.

The colour palette

Dreamweaver works with a set of standard web colours but there are lots more colour options available to you as the activity below demonstrates.

Activity 13: The colour palette...

In this activity you will:

● explore the choice of colours available in Dreamweaver.

▶ You can see a wide choice of colours by clicking on the **Text Color** icon in the **Properties** pane. There are 12 system colours in the first column and 216 web-safe colours in the grid to the right.

▶ You can change the palette by clicking on the right-arrow.

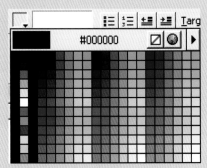

Figure 2.19: *The colours interface.*

This should be enough, but maybe the exact colour you need is not included. In this case, you will need to work with the **custom colour** list in the **System Color Picker** (click 🔘). You can choose the colour by *either*:

▶ clicking on the palette on the right of the **custom colour** interface and then clicking **OK** *or*

▶ entering specific values for:

- red
- green
- blue
- hue
- saturation
- luminosity.

In most cases, you would have to ask your client for these values. However, it is unlikely that most clients would know these, as it is quite specialist knowledge. The best thing to do is to get as close to the colour you need and hope that the client is happy with it!

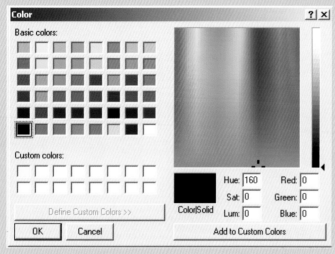

Figure 2.20: *The custom colour interface.*

Changing font colours

Now that you understand the range of colours which are available to you, we can look at how you may use these to suit the house style.

Font colours are applied in very much the same way as font styles and font sizes. The only real difference is that you will choose your colours from a visual display rather than a drop-down list.

Activity 14: Changing font colour…

In this activity you will:

● learn how to change a font colour.

▶ Start by either selecting where you want to work or by selecting a piece of text which has already been entered.

▶ Click on the **Text Color** icon.

▶ Choose the colour you wish to use, from the colour grid, the **System Color Picker** or by clicking anywhere that has the required colour (e.g. in an image).

▶ Any text you now type in (other than if you click in an area defined by a template) will be in the colour you have chosen. You should notice that the colour displayed in the **Properties** pane has changed to display the colour you have just chosen.

How does this apply to Sam's website?

You can now set the colour for the main body text.

Sam's design shows that the main body text has to be blue.

▶ Highlight the main body text and choose **blue** from the colour grid.

A final note about colour

When you are set a brief, you will probably be asked to use certain colours on your website. This is because many businesses have set colours which are usually associated with the business. When these colours are used, customers are then reminded of the business.

Text alignment

Text alignment is simply a process of choosing one of four settings and applying it to your text. You will probably have covered this in Key Stage 3 ICT lessons or elsewhere, but it is worth a reminder. There are four text alignments you could choose:

- **left aligned** – this means that text will sit on the left of a page or column so that, from a distance, it looks like a straight line has been drawn down the left of the page
- **right aligned** – this is the opposite of left aligned
- **centred** – all text is balanced along a central pivot, so that both left and right margins are jagged
- **fully justified** – text is set so that there is a straight line down the left and right margins (this can affect the spacing of text on a page).

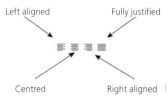

Figure 2.21: *The left, centred, right and fully justified icons.*

Each of these options is available by clicking on the relevant icon in the **Properties** pane.

How does this apply to Sam's website?

Sam's design shows that the main body text is to be fully justified.

You can now set the final design aspect to the main body text.

▶ Add some extra body text so that there are several lines.

▶ Select the main body text.

▶ Click the **Justify** button on the **Properties** pane.

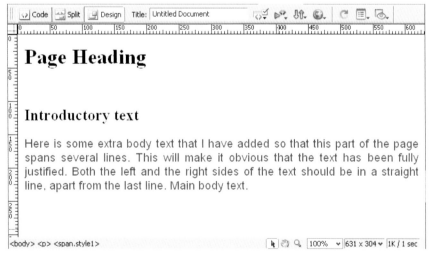

Figure 2.22: *The template with the main body text added and correctly formatted.*

Text attributes

The final piece of text on Sam's design is a motto at the bottom of the page. This uses the same font style and size as the main body text but is also in bold and is centred. Bold is one of three main attributes which you can apply to text. There are more but you will only really ever need the two shown below. We will now look at how you can set attributes to your text.

There are two icons on the **Properties** pane (and the **Text** toolbar) which you should use to set text attributes for any text you use:

These are simple and consistent to use. We are using **bold** as an example, although the method for use is very similar to how you set font styles and size earlier in the chapter. It is also possible to underline text, but Dreamweaver discourages this because people using your website are likely to think that underlined text is a hyperlink.

Figure
2.23: *Bold and italic icons.*

How does this apply to Sam's website?

▶ Move down two lines (hit **enter** twice on the keyboard).

▶ Click on the **Bold** icon to make the text bold.

▶ Click on the **centre** icon to set the text as being centrally aligned.

▶ Change the size and font.

▶ Add the motto:

Camp Freddy – here to blow the doors off!

> ⊘TIP
>
> There are two key combinations which you can use as shortcuts for setting text as bold or italic:
>
> • CTRL+B makes text bold
> • CTRL+I makes text italic.

Changing background colours

We have not quite finished with the template. In the following activity you will learn how to apply background colours. You may also be asked to complete the exercise on setting background images on page 40, although you would have to create a new website for this task.

The background colour for a page is set as one of the properties of a page. Page properties are all dealt with in the **Page Properties** dialogue box.

Activity 15: Changing background colours...

In this activity you will:

* learn how to change the background colour of a web page.

▶ Click on **Modify** on the main menu at the top of the page and click on **Page Properties**.

The **Page Properties** dialogue box should appear.

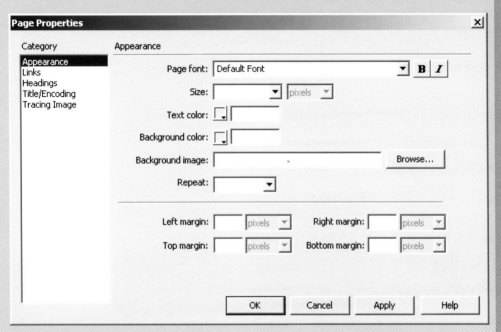

Figure 2.24: The Page Properties dialogue box.

This dialogue box allows you to change the settings for both the background of the current page **and** hyperlinks for that page. It also allows you to change font colour.

▶ Your current background colour will be shown in the square to the right of the **Background color** label. If no particular value has been set, the square will be grey.

▶ Click on the coloured square. The range of colour options will pop up, as explained above. Choose the colour you wish to use for your background and then click **OK**.

Your background colour will now be applied to your web page as a solid colour fill.

⊙TIP

The Page Properties dialogue box can also be accessed by right clicking anywhere on the page and choosing Page Properties from the menu which appears.

Key terms

Page properties

The title and other settings which apply to a page. Each page will have a different title and may have other unique settings, such as background.

Solid colour fill

This means that a solid block of colour, with no changes or shading, has been used to fill an area of a page. With backgrounds, this means that the whole of the page has been filled with one colour only.

How does this apply to Sam's website?

Sam's design shows that each page is to have a yellow background.

▶ Right click on your page and select **Page Properties** from the menu that appears.

▶ Make sure that the **Category** is set to **Appearance**.

▶ Click on the **Background color** square.

▶ Choose **yellow** from the palette which appears.

▶ Click **OK**.

Background images

The activity below is a very worthwhile exercise because it explores the use of images, rather than colours, as backgrounds. **However, if you are going to complete it, you will need to create a new website in Dreamweaver.** To avoid confusion, it may be better to come back to this exercise once you have completed your template.

If you explored the **Page Properties** dialogue box, you may have noticed that you can choose to use a background image for your web page. We will now look at how this can be used.

Activity 16: More backgrounds...

In this activity you will:

● experiment with using backgrounds other than solid colour fill.

You will be using **paris.jpg** for this exercise. This image is in the **images** folder you downloaded earlier. You will be using this image as the background for a web page.

You must be in the **Design** view to do this exercise.

▶ To set the image as your background, open the **Page Properties** dialogue box as before.

▶ Make sure that the **Appearance** category is selected in the list on the left.

(▶) Click the **Browse** button to the right of **Background image**.

(▶) Select and open the **images** folder.

(▶) Select **paris.jpg** and click **OK**.

(▶) Click **OK** to close the **Page Properties** dialogue box.

The background of your page should now have changed to show a section of the original image. The reason why you cannot see the whole of the image is that the picture is actually bigger than the page size. We will look at how you can change the size of an image to suit page size later in this book.

Adding an image to our template

Sam's design shows an image on every page, just below the main heading. This image should be 480 pixels wide and 360 pixels high. Dreamweaver allows you to add a fixed-size placeholder for an image.

About images

The first thing to say about images for websites is that if you want to guarantee that every web browser will be able to show your image, you must use one of the following three formats only:

- .gif
- .png
- .jpg

If you want to use images for your computer by drawing them on a software program free-hand, you should use the .gif format, especially if there are only a few colours used in the picture. The .gif format may also be used for animations. If you want to use photographs, you should use either the .png or .jpg format.

The second thing to say about images is that if the image you want to use is too big, you must resize it in an image manipulation package and then save it as a smaller image. For example, **paris.jpg** is too big for our needs at the moment and needs to be resized in an image manipulation package, which will make it quicker to download. We will discuss this again in the section on 'optimising images' towards the end of this chapter on page 51.

Activity 17: Inserting an image placeholder onto the template...

In this activity you will:

- insert an image placeholder onto the template.

(▶) Click on the blank line under the page heading.

(▶) Select **Insert...Image Objects...Image Placeholder** from the menu.

▶ The **Image Placeholder** dialogue box should appear. Enter **480** for the **Width** and **360** for the **Height** and press **OK**.

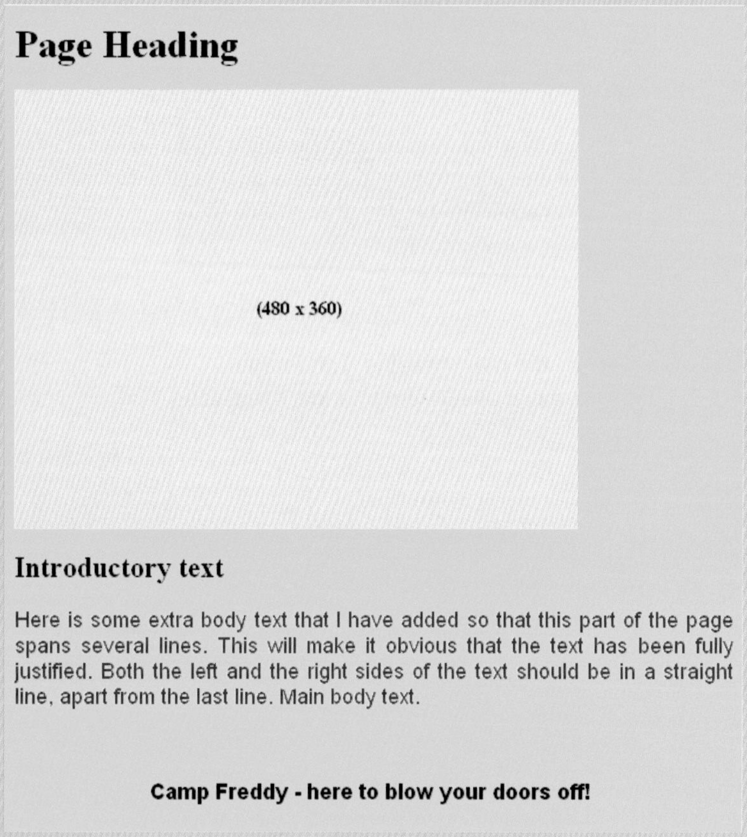

Page Heading

(480 x 360)

Introductory text

Here is some extra body text that I have added so that this part of the page spans several lines. This will make it obvious that the text has been fully justified. Both the left and the right sides of the text should be in a straight line, apart from the last line. Main body text.

Camp Freddy - here to blow your doors off!

Figure 2.25: *The template with an image placeholder added.*

Working with hyperlinks

Finally in this section, you will learn how to change the settings for hyperlinks. This is very much like changing the background colour in the previous section and is done using the same **Page Properties** dialogue box. You have not yet added any hyperlinks, so there will not be any changes shown on the page but, by setting the changes in your template, you will be making the settings for the pages you create.

Key terms

Hyperlinks

These are links to other web page locations. When you click on the hyperlink, you are taken to the new location.

Activity 18: Changing the settings for hyperlinks...

In this activity you will:

● learn how to change the settings for hyperlinks.

▶ Right click on the web page in **Design** view and select **Page Properties** from the menu which appears. The **Page Properties** dialogue box will now appear.

▶ Select the **Links** category. There are four boxes for setting hyperlink colours:

- ● link color
- ● visited links
- ● rollover links
- ● active links.

▶ Click on the **Link color** box and choose a green colour from the palette. Click **OK**.

Save the template

You have now added all the elements included in Sam's design for her website. You now need to save the template.

Activity 19: Saving a template...

In this activity you will:

● learn how to save your template.

▶ Select the page heading and then use **Insert...Template Objects...Editable Region** from the menu. Give it the name **Page Heading**.

▶ Repeat this for the image, introductory text, body text and motto.

▶ Click the **Code** button to view the HTML content of the page.

You will be able to see the grey **InstanceBeginEditable** and **InstanceEndEditable** comments that mark the beginning and end of the editable areas. You may find that the editable regions are all within paragraph HTML tags (i.e. there is a **<p align="justify">** immediately before the **InstanceBeginEditable** comment and a **</p>** immediately after the **InstanceEndEditable** one). This is fine for most of the editable areas, which will just contain text.

To allow more flexibility for the body text (and, in particular, to allow it to contain tables), you must put the paragraph tags inside the editable area so that they may be overwritten in pages based on the template.

▶ Make sure that the paragraph tags are inside the **Body Text** editable area. It should look something like this:

<!-- TemplateBeginEditable name="Body Text" --><p align="justify"><span class="style1">Here is some extra body text that I have added so that this part of the page spans several lines. This will make it obvious that the text has been fully justified. Both the left and the right sides of the text should be in a straight line, apart from the last line. Main body text.</span></p><!-- TemplateEndEditable -->

▶ Click **Design** to change back to design view, which should look the same as it did before.

▶ Click **File...Save**. The **Save As Template** dialogue box will now appear.

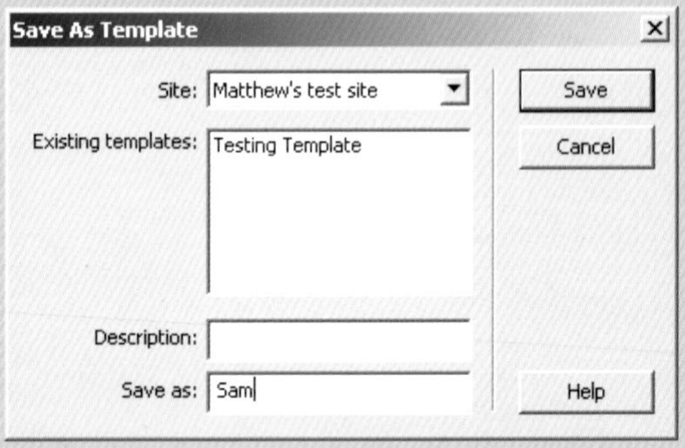

Save As Template

Site: Matthew's test site

Existing templates: Testing Template

Description:

Save as: Sam

Save
Cancel
Help

Figure 2.26: The Save As Template dialogue box.

▶ Name the template **Sam** and click **OK**.

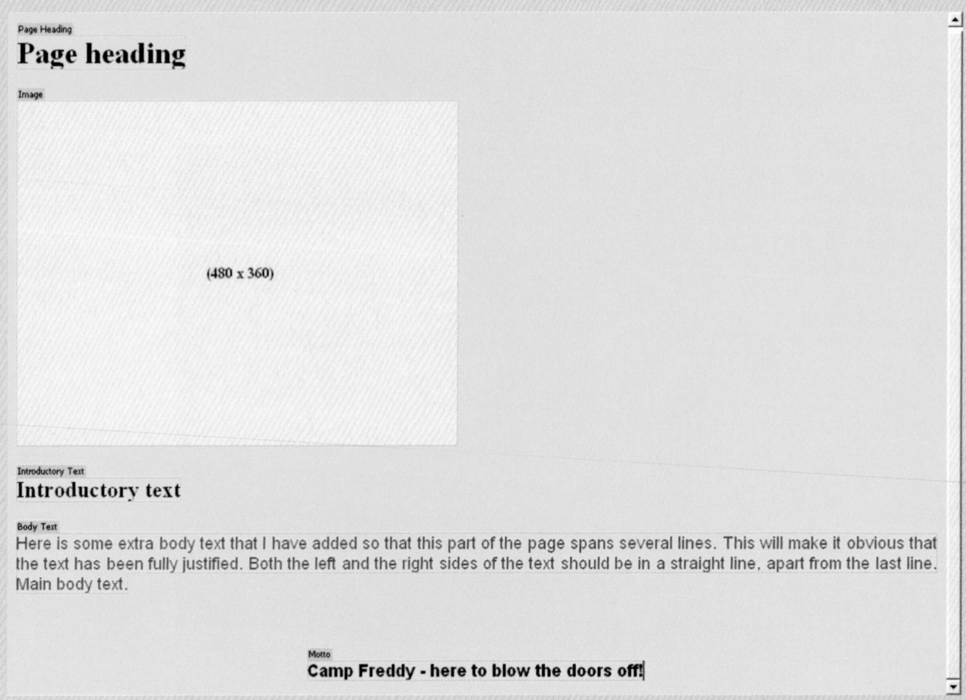

Page Heading

Page heading

Image

(480 x 360)

Introductory Text
Introductory text

Body Text
Here is some extra body text that I have added so that this part of the page spans several lines. This will make it obvious that the text has been fully justified. Both the left and the right sides of the text should be in a straight line, apart from the last line. Main body text.

Motto
Camp Freddy - here to blow the doors off!

Figure 2.27: The completed template.

Due to the amount of detail included in this template, a student who produced such a template in their own work would probably be working at a **Merit** level.

⊙TIP

Remember that the difference between a Pass template and a Merit template is the amount of detail. The more details that are set by your template, the more likely it is to achieve a Merit score.

Congratulations! You have now created the template you will use to create all of the pages in Sam's website.

Use the template to create the web pages for Sam's website

Follow the steps in the activity below to use the template to create the pages for Sam's website.

Activity 20: Creating website pages using a template...

In this activity you will:

- use your template to create the pages for Sam's website.

▶ Create a new page using **File...New** and clicking on the **Templates** tab. Select your site and the **Sam** template, and then click **Create**.

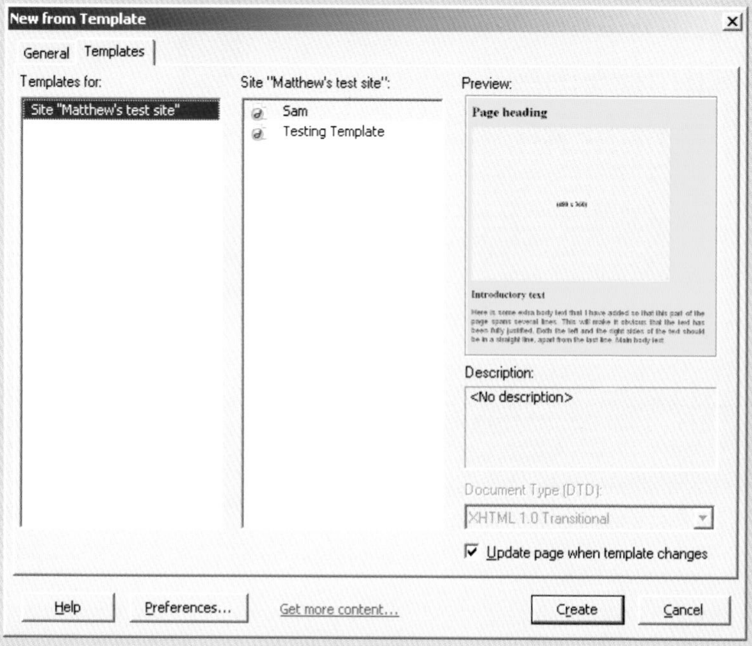

New from Template

General Templates

Templates for:

Site "Matthew's test site"

Site "Matthew's test site":

Sam
Testing Template

Preview:

Page heading

(488 x 300)

Introductory text

Here is some extra body text that I have added so that this part of the page spans several lines. This will make it obvious that the text has been fully justified. Both the left and the right sides of the text should be in a straight line, apart from the last line. Main body text

Description:

<No description>

Document Type (DTD):

XHTML 1.0 Transitional

☑ Update page when template changes

Help   Preferences...   Get more content...   Create   Cancel

Figure 2.28: *The New from Template dialogue box with the template you have created.*

▶ Repeat this process to create four more new pages.

Renaming web pages

Each new page that you have created in Activity 20 will have a name based on the Untitled-1 model (i.e. Untitled-2, Untitled-3 and so on). We have already discussed using descriptive filenames and so you need to change these names to suit those in Sam's website.

You may be surprised to see that the five pages you have just created for Sam's website are not shown in the **Files** list for your test site. This is because Dreamweaver treats each of these pages as a sort of prospective member of the website until they are saved. If you now close Dreamweaver, none of the pages you have just created will be saved. However, if you modify a page so that it differs from the template, Dreamweaver will ask you if you want to save the new page before allowing you to close it.

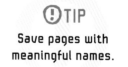
⏻TIP
Save pages with
meaningful names.

Activity 21: Renaming web pages...

In this activity you will:

- save and rename your web pages.

We have agreed that Untitled-1 is not a very descriptive name. As you are creating the first page, it makes sense that this should be the first web page that visitors get to see. You will probably know this as the homepage but, on most websites, this page will be saved as **index.html**. So, you need to change the name.

▶ Click on the **File** menu and choose **Save As**.

▶ Change the **File name** to **index.html** and click **Save**.

Notice that **index.html** appears in the **Files** list for your site.

You should now save each page you have just created. The remaining web pages in Sam's website are to be called:

- **members.html**
- **contact.html**
- **feedback.html**
- **futuregigs.html**

▶ Save and name the remaining four pages in Sam's website.

Key terms

Index or homepage

The homepage is what users call the first page of a website. When homepages are created by web authors, they are usually saved as index.htm or index.html.

Headings

Sam's original plans for her website show a heading for each page. These are shown in the table below.

Web page name	Heading
index.html	Welcome to the world of Camp Freddy!
members.html	Meet the band
contact.html	Get in contact
feedback.html	Fans feedback page
futuregigs.html	Look into the future!

Your template included a space to add a heading.

▶ Open each page and add the correct heading by clicking on the section which says **Page heading** and overwriting your prompt.

Introductory and additional text

When Sam asked you to create the website, she gave you some documents from which she wanted you to use some text. She also said that she was happy for you to create some text of your own. The three documents she has given you are as follows:

- **intros**
- **news release**
- **biographies**.

You should have downloaded these documents at the start of this chapter. If you have not had a chance to do so yet, now might be a good time! We will now add some introductory content from one of these documents and an article from another.

Activity 22: Adding text...

In this activity you will:

- add some introductory text to each web page
- add an article to one of the web pages.

  ▶ Open the word-processing file **intros**.

You will see that Sam has supplied you with an introduction for every page of her website and has also told you which page to use them on.

  ▶ Find the introductory text for the homepage.

  ▶ Open **index.html** in **Design** view.

  ▶ Click on the area of text which says **introductory text** and type in the text which Sam has given you.

  ▶ Repeat this process to add the introductory text for each of the pages of Sam's website.

Figure 2.29: *Futuregigs.html with heading and introductory text.*

Sam also gave you a document called **news release**. Sam wants you to use most of this document but not the second paragraph. She wants this to be the main article below introductory text on the **future gigs** page.

▶ Open the word-processing file **news release**.

▶ Select the heading and first paragraph by highlighting it with the mouse.

▶ Either choose **Edit…Copy** or use the shortcut **CTRL+C** to copy this section.

▶ Open the Dreamweaver website you have created for Sam and choose **futuregigs. html**.

▶ Move the cursor to the start of the **Body Text** section and press **enter**. This will create a new paragraph in the same style as the existing one.

▶ Use **Edit…Paste Special**, select **Text only** and press **OK**. The text you have selected should now appear on the page.

▶ Repeat this process to copy and paste the third paragraph onto the same page of Sam's website.

▶ Delete the original paragraph of body text.

Using tables

Your website is now beginning to really take shape but you are probably wondering about the layout of pages. If you look at the design for **members.html**, you will see that this page is laid out in tables. Tables are a really useful way of laying out a page.

> ⊘TIP
>
> **You can use CSS to control the layout of a page, as well as the formatting of its elements. However, the syllabus for this course specifically mentions using tables for layout, so you should use this rather than CSS (you can still use CSS for formatting – see page 56).**

Creating the layout for the members page

In the activity below you will create the layout for the **members** page. The design for this page shows that all of the information included on this page is set out in a three-column table. Column 1 shows the band member's name, column 2 shows their photograph and column 3 holds their biography. You will also notice that the table will hold an icon which will be used as a hyperlink to an external website. This table replaces the main body text for this page.

Activity 23: Creating a table…

In this activity you will:

● add a table to the members page.

▶ Open the page **members.html**.

▶ Select and delete the **Body Text** content.

(▶) Your cursor should now be in the **Body Text** box. If not, click there now.

(▶) Click on **Insert…Table**. This will bring up the **Table** dialogue box.

(▶) Choose **7** rows and **3** columns.

(▶) Change the **Table width** to **100** and select **percent** from the drop-down list beside it.

(▶) Click **OK** to create your table.

You should now have a table with three columns and seven rows. Each row and each column should be the same size.

(▶) You will now insert the names of each member of the band as well as the instrument they play in the first column of the table. These are:

- Sam, lead singer and keyboard
- Jon, backing vocals and rhythm guitar
- Matt, lead guitar
- Tom, drums
- Lenny, bass

(▶) Add these details to each cell in the left column. Each band member should be on their own row. When you have finished, there should be two rows which have not been used.

(▶) The second column will be used for a photograph, so leave this blank. The third column will hold details about each band member. These details are currently held in the file called **biographies**. You should now open this file and copy the text for each band member into the correct space in the table. As you add text, the table will expand to hold the added text.

(▶) Click and drag your mouse from the top-left to the bottom-right cell of the table to select them all. Select the blue body text style (probably called **style 1**) from the **Style** list in the **Properties** pane. All of the table's text should become blue to fit Sam's design.

Introductory Text

All five of us got together to write this page. We started by each member writing their own story, but Matt's went on about sausages and beans too much, so we then decided to each write someone else's piece. Mention is still made of sausage and beans on Matt's section, but trust us, there is less than if Matt had written it!

100% (394)

Sam, lead singer and keyboard	Sam has been singing in bands since she was 14. She started at school with some mates from her class. This band did the usual end of year gigs but did not survive the big break up at the end of year eleven. She then went on to sing for many different bands, but always wanted to write and perform her own songs. Camp Freddy has given her the chance to do this.	
Jon, backing vocals and rhythm guitar	Well, Jon. When not pulling cross eyes or driving everyone crazy with his stupid jokes, he does a great job of keeping the rhythm going. His pet hates include jams in A and sponge. When not playing guitar, he fits a mean kitchen.	
Matt, lead guitar	Matt is one of those guitarists who will play a song backwards, just to prove he can. We should all hate him because he does this sort of thing all the time, but he does it so well, and is such a nice bloke, we are all used to it. Other than playing guitar, his next love is sausage and beans.	
Tom, drums	Tom's mum says he was drumming since for ever, but that's a long long time. He sure can count to four and sometimes does it twice in a row, which is nice. Excellent use of snare is guaranteed to enhance any version of **"snake bite love"** and his sense of humour goes a long way to making Jon easier to deal with.	
Lenny, bass	This man puts Bass in its place! None of that jazz funk rubbish of yesteryear, just straight forward driving bass, played as though the man has a metronome for a head. Awesome. Watch him support Martin on **"I like sponge, but my baby just loves to dance"**. Pure joy.	

Figure 2.30: Members.html.

Using tables to set layout

The instructions for this unit explain that you should use tables to help lay out the elements for a web page. You have already started this process with the activity above, which uses a table with a border to help lay out elements. The activity below looks at using a table without visible borders.

Activity 24: Creating a table without visible borders...

In this activity you will:

- create a table to help arrange elements on a web page
- set the table border size to 0.

You have been asked to set up a web page holding a list of products and prices. You decide that the best way of setting this out on a page is to have a list of products down the left of the page and the prices down the right. You could do this using tabs, but this is both inefficient and unreliable. You will now create a two-column, two-row table to show how this could be done more efficiently.

▶ Open a blank web page not based on any template.

▶ Click on **Insert...Table** to create a table on this page. Do not click **OK** yet!

▶ Set the **Border thickness** to 0 pixels.

▶ Now click **OK**.

Your table has now been created so that you can use the individual cells as layout guides, but the table does not have any visible borders, so all the viewer sees is a well-laid-out web page.

Extension

Here are some extra tricks you could use when creating a table.

▶ Try clicking with the left button of your mouse on the border between the first and second columns and, while holding the button down, dragging the border to the left. This will change the width of both columns.

▶ Try selecting a cell of a table and creating another table inside this cell. This will give you even greater control over the layout.

Proof!

How can you prove you have created a table which no one can see? If you look at the table in **Design** view, you can see that Dreamweaver shows where the table is by using dotted lines. A screenshot of this page with all text and images added, and with dotted lines to show where the table is, would be good evidence that you have created and used a table to help layout.

How does this apply to Sam's website?

You will have seen that each page on the website has a one-row, four-column table at the bottom below the motto. This table will be used to hold hyperlinks from each page of the website to the other four pages. Because this table is on every page, you should add it to the template.

▶ Open the **sam.dwt** template.

▶ In **Design** view, below the motto at the bottom, insert a table with **1** row and **4** columns, scaled to **100 percent** and without a border.

▶ Click in each of the four table cells in turn, using **Insert…Template Objects… Editable Region** to create placeholders for the hyperlinks. Name them **Navigation Link 1** to **Navigation Link 4**.

▶ In **Code** view, ensure that the four columns are the same width by changing each of the **<td>** tags to **<td width="25%">**.

▶ Save the template. The **Update Template Files** dialogue box should appear, listing the five pages in Sam's website. Click **Update**.

▶ Check that the five pages of the website have the empty table at the bottom.

⊙TIP

The assessment grid for this unit makes it clear that you must use some tables to help with the layout of your website for a Merit grade for this assessment objective and must use tables throughout for a Distinction grade.

We are now going to look at the use of:

* images
* animations
* interactive elements
* video
* sound.

Images

Optimising images

When you open a web page, all of the code for that web page is sent to your computer and then your web browser uses this code to reconstruct the web page on your screen. If the web page also includes images, these have to be downloaded before they can be seen. This explains why some websites take longer to open than others, especially if you are using a dial-up connection to access the Internet.

We have already mentioned changing the size of an image in image manipulation software rather than just resizing it on a page. This is because any image which is used is first down-loaded and then placed on a page. This means that the same image size is downloaded if the image has been resized in Dreamweaver to look like a thumbnail, or has been made bigger to fill the whole of a background. The process of changing the file size of an image by resizing it in an image manipulation package is called **optimising**.

If you are targeting either a **Merit** or a Distinction for this unit, you must show that you have optimised images. For a **Merit** grade, you must provide screenshots which show that *some* images have been optimised, while for a Distinction grade, you must show that *all* images have been optimised.

Activity 25: Optimising images...

In this activity you will:

- optimise **paris.jpg** for use on your website.

▶ Open your image manipulation software. This will need to be a reasonably sophisticated program, such as Paint Shop Pro, rather than Microsoft Paint.

▶ Navigate to **paris.jpg**. Open this image.

▶ Use your menu to find the **resize** tool. Open this tool to change the size of **paris.jpg** so that the width is 400 pixels and the height 300 pixels.

▶ Save your image as **webparis.jpg**.

Key terms

Thumbnail images

Small versions of large pictures which, when clicked on, usually open up a larger version of the same image.

Optimising

Changing the file size of an element, such as an image, so that page download times are kept to a minimum.

Adding images

You have already added an image placeholder to your template. You will now add the actual images to your pages.

Activity 26: Adding images...

In this activity you will:

- add images to your web pages.

You need to use five of the .jpg files you have stored in your **images** folder. These are:

- **1.jpg**
- **2.jpg**
- **3.jpg**
- **4.jpg**
- **5.jpg**

▶ Use image manipulation software to change the size of each image to 480 pixels wide by 360 pixels high.

▶ Open **index.html**.

▶ Right click the image placeholder and select **Source File** from the menu that appears.

▶ Navigate to **1.jpg**, select it and click **OK**. **1.jpg** will appear on the page.

▶ Follow this procedure to add **2.jpg** to **members.html**, **3.jpg** to **contact.html**, **4.jpg** to **feedback.html** and **5.jpg** to **futuregigs.html**.

You have also been given five other .jpg files:

- **Sam.jpg**
- **Jon.jpg**
- **Matt.jpg**
- **Tom.jpg**
- **Lenny.jpg**

These are to be used on the **members** page.

▶ Each image is a different size. Use image manipulation software to change the size of each image to 240 pixels wide by 160 pixels high.

▶ Add each image to the relevant cell in the table on the **members** page by using **Insert…Image**.

Introductory Text

All five of us got together to write this page. We started by each member writing their own story, but Matt's went on about sausages and beans too much, so we then decided to each write someone else's piece. Mention is still made of sausage and beans on Matt's section, but trust us, there is less than if Matt had written it!

100% (994)

Sam, lead singer and keyboard		Sam has been singing in bands since she was 14. She started at school with some mates from her class. This band did the usual end of year gigs but did not survive the big break up at the end of year eleven. She then went on to sing for many different bands, but always wanted to write and perform her own songs. Camp Freddy has given her the chance to do this.
Jon, backing vocals and rhythm guitar		Well, Jon. When not pulling cross eyes or driving everyone crazy with his stupid jokes, he does a great job of keeping the rhythm going. His pet hates include jams in A and sponge. When not playing guitar, he fits a mean kitchen.

Figure 2.31: *Members page completed.*

Animation

You have also been given an animation for use on the website. This is called **anim.gif**. Animations are added in exactly the same way as images. This file is to be inserted below the introductory text on **contacts.html**. You may have noticed that this page also uses a table to help with its layout.

Activity 27: Adding animations...

In this activity you will:

- add an animation to one of your web pages.

▶ Open **contacts.html**.

▶ Delete the **Body Text** content. Add a two-column, two-row table with border size 0 which is 50% of the width of the page.

▶ Insert the animation **anim.gif** as shown on the original plan for the page.

Video

Videos are added to web pages in much the same way as pictures. Before you add a video to a page, you need to decide whether you want the video to run when the page is accessed or when a visitor moves a mouse over the file, as both of these options can be set when you add a video to a page.

Activity 28: Inserting a video...

In this activity you will:

- add a video to one of your web pages.

▶ Choose where on the web page you want the video to go.

▶ Click on **Insert...Media...Flash** in the main menu. This is the option to use for **.swf** files, which are the easiest type of video to add.

▶ Navigate to **live.swf**, select it and click **OK**.

▶ Add a title if you like, then click **OK**.

A placeholder for the video appears on the page. When it is selected, you can change its attributes in the **Properties** pane. In particular, if **Loop** is ticked then the video will start again from the beginning when it reaches the end, and if **Autoplay** is ticked then the video will automatically start to play once the page loads. You can use the **Play** button to view the video.

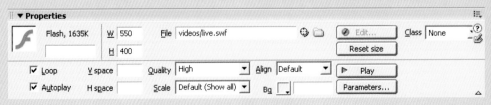

Figure 2.32: The Properties pane.

How does this apply to Sam's website?

Live is a video file which needs to be added to **futuregigs.html**.

▶ The location of this video is shown on the original plan on page 11.

▶ This video should be set to play as soon as the web page is opened and to not loop.

Sound

A sound file in .wav format can be added as a background sound for a web page.

Activity 29: Adding sound...

In this activity you will:

● add a sound file to your index web page.

You have been given a sound file **track8** to add as the background to **index.html**. This sound file should be in the **music** folder.

▶ Open **index.html**.

▶ Delete everything from the **Body Text** box.

▶ Use **Insert...Media...Plugin** from the main menu. The **Select File** dialogue box should appear.

▶ Navigate to **track8.wma**, select it and click **OK**.

▶ An icon appears in the page. Drag its bottom-right corner to resize it to about the same width as the image above it and about one and a half times its original height.

▶ Use **File...Preview in Browser** and select **Internet Explorer** from the list. Internet Explorer should load and display the page. If the music doesn't start playing automatically, click the security banner at the top of Internet Explorer and then click **Allow Blocked Content**.

Notice that users can use the controls on the embedded player to stop the music or to change its volume.

About interactive elements

Interactive elements are items on a web page which require the user to click or select or move the mouse over them before something happens. The embedded sound you inserted above may be considered an interactive element. If you are able to use more complicated HTML code, which is beyond the scope of this book, or wish to experiment with adding plug-ins to your page, you may be able to add further interactive elements.

Using cascading style sheets for Sam's website

Distinction candidates will have been very patient while waiting for the section on how to create the cascading style sheets you must use if you are to be awarded a **Distinction** grade for Assessment Objective 2. We will now look at how cascading style sheets can be created and used in your website.

Creating the cascading style sheet for Sam's website

You will remember that cascading style sheets are applied by editing the HTML code for a web page. Follow the steps in the activity below to create a cascading style sheet and then a new website using this sheet.

You were reminded on page 30 about the design requirements for Sam's website. If you are unclear, go back now and remind yourself of the designs shown in the first chapter. Because of the increased potential of cascading style sheets to do things relatively easily, you will be adding slightly more using a cascading style sheet than if you were just using a template to control the formatting. This would seem to fit the needs of the **Distinction** level!

Activity 30: Creating a cascading style sheet for Sam's website…

In this activity you will:

- enter code to create a cascading style sheet for Sam's website.

▶ Use **File…New** to open the **New Document** dialogue box.

▶ Make sure that the **General** tab is on display, and select **CSS Style Sheets** as the **Category**.

▶ Click **Create** (it doesn't matter which style sheet template is selected in the second list).

▶ In **Code** view, select all the text and delete it.

▶ Enter the following code:

body {background-color: yellow; font-family: "Times New Roman", Times, serif; font-size: medium; color: blue}

h1 {color: red; font-family: Arial, Helvetica, sans-serif; font-size: xx-large}

h2 {color: red; font-family: Arial, Helvetica, sans-serif; font-size: x-large}

a {text-decoration: none; font-style: italic; text-transform: lowercase}

a:link { color: red; font-weight: bold}

a:visited { color: blue}

a:hover { color: green; text-transform: uppercase}

a:active { color: green}

This sets up the background colour as well as the settings for Heading 1, Heading 2 and the default body text. It also sets unvisited hyperlinks to red, and visited hyperlinks to blue. As the mouse hovers over a link, the link becomes upper-case and green. This is an example of using the cascading style sheet to add an interactive element to your website and shows the advantage of using a cascading style sheet because, once set here, every hyperlink will have the same rollover effect.

TIP

HTML uses American spellings! Watch out for the word *color* especially.

 Save your cascading style sheet as **Sam.css**.

Applying the cascading style sheet to Sam's website

The syllabus for this course indicates that candidates should use CSS instead of a template if they are to achieve a **Distinction** grade. However, a template can mean different things, from a copy of an existing HTML page to the sophisticated templates with editable regions that Dreamweaver supports.

It is unlikely that you will be penalised for using Dreamweaver templates to add fixed content, such as navigation links, to your pages – after all, this is exactly what professional web designers do. However, it is important, if you are aiming for a **Distinction** grade, that you demonstrate that all of the formatting has been applied using CSS.

Activity 31: Applying the cascading style sheet to Sam's website...

In this activity you will:

● apply your cascading style sheet to Sam's website.

▶ Open the template **Sam.dwt** in **Code** view.

▶ Delete the following lines from the file (these represent the manual changes you made to the background and hyperlink colours):

```
body {
    background-color: #FFFF00;
}
a:link {
    color: #006600;
}
```

▶ Click **Design**. Your template should now have a white background (the default).

(▶) Back in **Code** view, insert the following HTML code at the very end of the <head> section. (This should be the line above the </head> tag. You will need to insert a new, blank line to insert this code. The **..** shows that the css file is in the parent folder of the template.)

```
<link rel="stylesheet" href="../Sam.css" />
```

(▶) Click **Design**. The background should be yellow again, and this time the headings should be red. This formatting is controlled by the cascading style sheet you have just linked to.

There are still a couple of styles embedded in the template itself (probably called **style1** and **style2**). It would be tidier to move these to the external style sheet.

(▶) Cut the following lines (or their equivalents) from **Sam.dwt** and paste them into **Sam.css**:

```
.style1 {
    font-family: Arial, Helvetica, sans-serif;
    font-size: 14pt;
    color: #0000FF;
}
.style2 {
    font-family: Arial, Helvetica, sans-serif;
    font-size: 14pt;
}
```

TIP

In your own websites, you should rename any styles you create so that they have more meaningful names than style1, style2, etc.

(▶) You should be left with an empty style section in **Sam.dwt**, so you can delete these lines:

```
<style type="text/css">
<!--

-->
</style>
```

(▶) Save the template and update the pages in the site.

Finishing touches

- The image **link.jpg** on **members.html** is used as a hyperlink. You should insert this image ready for it to be set up as a hyperlink in the next chapter.
- Similarly, the invitation to send in emails on **contact.html** should be added. This is a piece of body text. Do not add the text for the actual email link as you will add this in the next chapter.

CHAPTER

→ Assessment Objective 3

Create Functioning Hyperlinks

Overview:

In this chapter you will be shown how to create a range of hyperlinks to use in your website. Some of these hyperlinks will be to pages in your own website, while others should be to external websites. You should also include hyperlinks to email.

> In order to complete the activities in this chapter you will need access to a number of additional files. These files are contained in the Unit 2 Resources zip file which can be downloaded from the OCR Nationals in ICT (Units 2 & 20) Student Resources page on the Payne-Gallway website: www.payne-gallway.co.uk.

How this assessment objective will be assessed...

You will be assessed on the following aspects of your hyperlinks:

- how well you link all pages in your website together
- the method of navigation you use
- the structure of your website navigation system
- the amount of links to external websites and email links you include
- whether you have used hotspots or image maps
- the relevance and consistency of the hyperlinks you use.

Skills to use...

- You will need to link all pages in your website together using a well-planned and consistent navigation system. Your work would probably benefit from some time spent looking at other websites to discover their methods of navigation. You may even pick up some design tips.
- You will need to keep a sense of purpose when you create and choose your hyperlinks.

How to achieve...

> **Pass requirements**
> **P1** You will link together all five pages in your website.
> **P2** The links used may not follow a consistent style.
> **P3** There will be at least one link to an external website.

Merit requirements

M1 You will link together all web pages.

M2 All links used will follow a consistent style and will show a clear structure.

M3 The website will include a link to an external website, as well as at least one email link and one hotspot/image map link.

Distinction requirements

D1 You will link together all web pages.

D2 All links used will follow a consistent style and be consistently located to create an easy-to-use and fully functioning system.

D3 The website will include links to a range of external websites, as well as email links and the use of hotspots and image map links.

What is a hyperlink?

Hyperlinks were explained in the last chapter but it is worthwhile reviewing them quickly. A hyperlink is something on a web page which, when you click on it, takes you to another web page, or maybe just to a place on the same web page.

But there is a little more! A hyperlink is something you click on to take you somewhere else but the great thing is how flexible websites can be. You can literally use any element on a web page as a hyperlink. This includes text, buttons, images and even areas of images. We will start by looking at how to create simple hyperlinks and then we will build up to creating more complicated ones later in this chapter.

The practice assignment

You have now created a website for Sam and her band. You will continue to work on the website in this chapter. Sam's design shows that she wants:

- text links
- one hyperlink attached to a small image
- an email link.

Textual hyperlinks are probably the simplest to create but this is not a problem – assessment of Assessment Objective 3 is based on **relevance** and **consistency**. Your website will not be marked down for this assessment objective providing there is a good reason to use mainly text links and as long as they are used on every page and always placed in the same logical position.

So that you can practise creating other types of hyperlink, you will be given small practice tasks during the chapter. These will not be based on Sam's website.

Planning the hyperlinks to and from each page

The original design for Sam's website showed that she wanted to use a **mesh structure** for her website. To create this structure, we will now add a link from every page on the website to all other pages in the website. These will all be placed in the cells of the table you added to the bottom of every web page.

Activity 1: Planning the hyperlinks from each page...

In this activity you will:

● plan hyperlinks from each page on Sam's website so that each page includes a link to all other pages in the website.

Sam wants to have a mesh structure for her website. You have created a website for Sam which has five pages.

Copy the table below and complete it to show the hyperlinks from each page. The first row has been done for you.

Page	Contains hyperlinks to:
index.html	members.html contact.html feedback.html futuregigs.html
members.html	
contact.html	
feedback.html	
futuregigs.html	

Adding the textual hyperlinks to index.html

Now you need to add textual hyperlinks between web pages on your website. Follow the steps below to add these links.

Activity 2: Adding the textual hyperlinks to index.html...

In this activity you will:

● create textual hyperlinks to web pages on your website.

▶ Open **index.html** in **Design** view.

▶ Scroll down to the bottom of the page, just below the motto. You should find a table waiting there just for this very activity. The plan for this is shown below.

Design for Sam's website

Hyperlinks table (at bottom of each page)

Band members page	Contact us	Leave some feedback	Upcoming gigs

All text to be 4(14), ARIAL, BLUE.
This is the plan for Index.html Other pages to have links to all the other pages of the web site.

Figure 3.1: The design plan for the hyperlinks table.

▶ You will work from left to right, adding a link from each cell of this table. Click on the first cell and replace the text with the following:

Band members page

▶ Select this text so that this becomes the hyperlink. Click on **Insert…Hyperlink**. The **Hyperlink** dialogue box will come up.

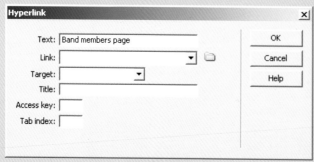

Figure 3.2: *The Hyperlink dialogue box.*

▶ Click the folder icon to the right of the **Link** label.

▶ Navigate to **members.html**, select it and click **OK**.

▶ Press **OK** on the **Hyperlink** dialogue box to apply the change.

You have now created your first hyperlink. This will take the structure set either by the template you are using or the CSS file you have applied to the page.

▶ Continue to add hyperlinks from **index.html** to the remaining three pages in your website.

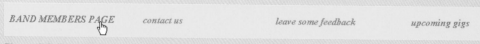

Figure 3.3: *Index.html showing the hyperlinks you have added.*

▶ Use **File…Preview in browser** to check the appearance of your hyperlinks.

⊙TIP

The links may not appear in red if you have previously viewed the pages in your web browser. You can clear your browser's history (Tools…Internet Options…Clear History in Internet Explorer) to check that the formatting of unvisited hyperlinks is as expected.

Adding links from other pages

Activity 3: Adding links from other pages...

In this activity you will:

● add a similar set of links from all of the other pages on your website. The link to each page must be exactly the same wherever it is used. The text for each link is shown in the table below.

Target web page	Text link
index.html	Homepage
members.html	Band members page
contact.html	Contact us
feedback.html	Leave some feedback
futuregigs.html	Upcoming gigs

▶ Create all of the necessary links on Sam's website.

⊘TIP

The assessment grid for Assessment Objective 3 states that hyperlinks should have a clear structure and be consistently located. By using a table to help plan your layout, these hyperlinks are consistently located. The use of clear and descriptive titles for each hyperlink gives the navigation system a clear structure.

⊘TIP

You could add all of the navigation links to the template. If you assign a different class attribute to each of them then you can override this using CSS embedded in the pages — for example, to make the Contact us link bold on the contact.html page only.

Adding the image hyperlink to Sam's website

The design for Sam's website shows that she wants a graphical link with a rollover effect from the members web page to the iTunes website. When created, this hyperlink will be an **external link**. You have been given an image file called **link.jpg** to use for this hyperlink. This should be in your **images** folder.

Activity 4: Adding an image hyperlink...

In this activity you will:

● create image hyperlinks to web pages on your website.

▶ Open the web page **members.html** in **Design** view.

▶ Move down to the seventh row of the table on this page. Choose the cell in column 3.

▶ Insert **link.jpg** into this cell from the **images** folder (you will have done this already if you're using a cascading style sheet). Centre this image in the cell.

▶ Select **link.jpg** by clicking on it.

▶ Type **http://www.apple.com/itunes/** into the **Link** area in the **Properties** pane.

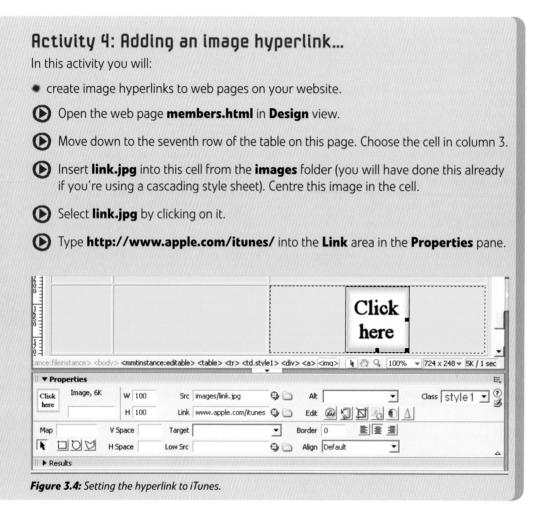

Figure 3.4: *Setting the hyperlink to iTunes.*

Adding an email link from Sam's website to your email address

You need to add an email link to your website if you are aiming for either a **Merit** or a **Distinction** grade for Assessment Objective 3. This email link *must* go to your email account. Luckily, this is very much like adding any other form of hyperlink.

The email link needs to be placed on the **contacts** page.

Activity 5: Adding an email link from a website to an email address...

In this activity you will:

● add an email link to your website.

(▶) Open the web page **contacts.html** in **Design** view.

(▶) Select the left-hand cell of the second row of the table above the motto. Add the following text to this cell:

   Feel free to email us!

This text should be in bold and centred within the cell.

(▶) Choose the right-hand cell of this row.

(▶) Click **Insert...Email Link**. The **Email Link** dialogue box will appear.

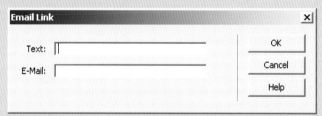

Figure 3.5: *The Email Link dialogue box.*

(▶) Sam has asked that you use the text **Click here to email us**. Add this to the **Text** box.

(▶) Type your email address in the **E-Mail** box.

(▶) Click **OK** to add your email link.

You have now created all of the hyperlinks needed to fit Sam's design. You should now save and close Sam's website.

Other types of hyperlink

You should now understand how to add hyperlinks to and from web pages within your website.

You will need to create a new HTML page to practise the skills included in the rest of this chapter. While these are not used for Sam's website, you should plan to use at least some of them for the website you create in response to the brief you are set for this unit.

Hotspots/image maps

Hotspots or image maps are a great way of adding hyperlinks to a page, as they allow you to set up links from sections of an image. Imagine you wanted to have an image which showed a range of books. You might want a web user to be able to click on the book and then be taken to a review of that book. Sounds good, doesn't it? Hotspots let you do this.

You will need the following files for Activity 6:

- **books.jpg**
- **book1.htm**
- **book2.htm**

Activity 6: Creating a hotspot...

In this activity you will:

- create a hotspot.

▶ Open a new blank web page in **Design** view. Insert **books.jpg** onto the page (you may have to resize it to fit). Save the page.

▶ Click the arrow beside the **Images** icon on the **Common** toolbar to display a menu of options, including hotspots.

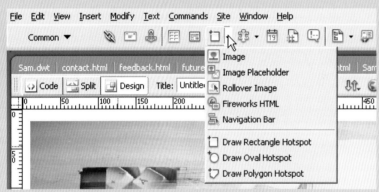

Figure 3.6: *The Images menu on the Common toolbar.*

▶ Use the **Rectangle**, **Oval** or **Polygon** hotspot tool to create a hotspot around the book on the left of the image.

▶ Click the **Browse for File** (folder) icon in the Properties pane and select **book1.htm**.

▶ Create a link to **book2.htm** from a hotspot created over the right-hand book.

▶ Test your hotspots by previewing the page in your web browser.

Navigation bars

You will need the following files for Activity 7:

- **button 1.jpg**
- **button 2.jpg**
- **button 3.jpg**
- **button 4.jpg**

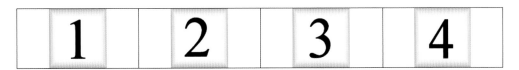

Figure 3.7: *A navigation bar.*

Activity 7: Creating a navigation bar...

In this activity you will:

- create a navigation bar like the one shown in Figure 3.7.

▶ Open a new blank web page in **Design** view.

▶ Click **Insert...Image Objects...Navigation Bar**. The **Insert Navigation Bar** dialogue box will appear.

▶ Change the **Element name** to **BBC** (note that element names cannot contain spaces).

▶ For the **Up image**, browse for **button 1.jpg**.

▶ Set the **Alternate text** to **BBC homepage**.

▶ Type the URL **http://www.bbc.co.uk** into the box below.

▶ Click the **Add item** button (the **+** at the top of the dialogue box).

▶ Repeat the above steps so that your navigation bar ends up with four elements – one each for **button 1.jpg**, **button 2.jpg**, **button 3.jpg** and **button 4.jpg** – linking to the websites of your choice.

▶ Click **OK** to create the navigation bar.

▶ Test your navigation bar by previewing your new page in your web browser.

Menus

Just like in a restaurant or café, menus bring all of the choices together in one list so that the viewer can make decisions more easily.

You have already created a simple menu for Sam's website by adding links to a table.

You can add more sophisticated menus, such as drop-down menus, by using JavaScript. This is beyond the scope of this book, but you should be able to search the web to find lots of example menu scripts that you can adapt for your own website.

Create Interactive Elements

Overview:

In this chapter, you will be shown how to create image and button rollovers which you can use to make your website appear more exciting. We will also look at other interactive elements which you can add to your website.

> In order to complete the activities in this chapter you will need access to an additional file. This file is contained in the Unit 2 Resources zip file which can be downloaded from the OCR Nationals in ICT (Units 2 & 20) Student Resources page on the Payne-Gallway website: www.payne-gallway.co.uk.

How this assessment objective will be assessed...

You will be assessed on the following aspects of your user form:

* the amount of different interactive elements you use
* the consistency you show in your work.

Skills to use...

* To pass this assessment objective, you will need to know how to create or import at least a rollover effect. For a **Merit**, you will need to create or import a wider range of different interactive elements, some of which you create yourself.
* **Distinction** candidates will need to use a limited amount of scripting (this will be awarded marks even though it may not always work).

How to achieve...

Pass requirements

P1 You will include one or more rollover images/buttons.

P2 You will identify all interactive elements of the completed website either on your printout or verbally to the VM.

Merit requirements

M1 You will include at least two rollover objects.

M2 You will use one other interactive element in your website.

M3 You will identify all interactive elements on your printout of the completed website.

Distinction requirements

D1   You will include at least three rollover objects.

D2   You will adopt a consistent approach to the design of button rollovers.

D3   There will be some limited use of scripting (HTML, Java, CGI), but this may not always work as intended.

What is an interactive element?

An interactive element is one which reacts when the user does something to it. This could be clicking on the element with the mouse or even moving the mouse over the element. You could argue that **hyperlinks** and the **submit** button on the form are both interactive. The hyperlink needs the user to click on it before anything happens and the submit button needs to be clicked before the form is sent off. Strictly speaking, you are correct. However, for this qualification, these types of interactive elements are awarded elsewhere, so we will look at some further examples here.

Types of interactive element

The interactive elements you could use are:

- rollovers
- Flash objects
- interactive buttons
- user controls
- specialist script languages (such as JavaScript and Java).

Rollovers

Key terms

Rollover

The effect where one image replaces another as the mouse moves over it.

You must include at least one rollover if you want to be awarded a Pass for Assessment Objective 4. If you want a Distinction, you will need to include three rollovers. If you have used a cascading style sheet to create Sam's website, you will already have created one rollover, which changes a hyperlink as the mouse moves over it.

Activity 1: Adding a rollover button to Sam's website...

In this activity you will:

● set up an image hyperlink on Sam's website.

When clicked, this takes the viewer from the member's page to the iTunes website. The design for Sam's website shows that this image should have a rollover effect attached to it. The alternative image is called **altim.jpg** and should be in your **images** folder.

▶ Open **members.html** in **Design** view.

▶ Click on **link.jpg** (the image you have used for the link to iTunes). This will select the image. Press **Delete**.

▶ Click **Insert...Image Objects...Rollover Image** to open the **Insert Rollover Image** dialogue box.

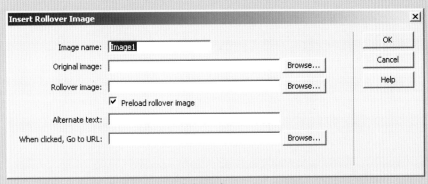

Figure 4.1: *The Insert Rollover Image dialogue box.*

▶ Set the **Original image** to **link.jpg**.

▶ Set the **Rollover image** to **altim.jpg**.

▶ Set the **URL** to **http://www.apple.com/itunes**.

Your completed dialogue box will be like the one shown below.

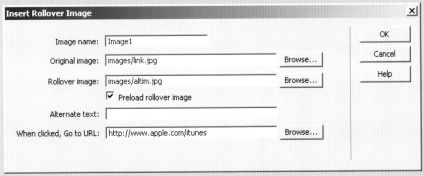

Figure 4.2: *The completed Insert Rollover Image dialogue box.*

▶ Save your page.

▶ Use **File...Preview in Browser** to test your button.

If you get an error about an unterminated string constant, check the code of your page. Inside the body, if the onmouseover part ends with ,') [comma, apostrophe, closing parenthesis] then change it to ,1) [comma, one, closing parenthesis]. This seems to be a bug in Dreamweaver.

We will now discuss the remaining interactive elements. These will not be used on Sam's website. However, you should consider using them on the website you create.

Flash buttons

Flash is a separate piece of software which could be the subject of a whole book on its own. If you know how to use Flash, then you will know how to create interactive elements, such as rollovers and other great effects. However, if you do not know how to use this software, Chapters 9 to 11 will serve as a good introduction.

Activity 2: Creating a Flash button...

In this activity you will:

● add a Flash button to a page.

▶ Create a new blank HTML page, save it with an appropriate name, and switch to **Design** view.

▶ Use **Insert...Media...Flash Button**. The **Insert Flash Button** dialogue box will appear.

▶ Click on each of the styles in turn to see what is on offer, then pick your favourite.

▶ Fill in the fields for **Button text** and **Link** and give your button an appropriate file name in the **Save as** box.

▶ Click **OK** to create the button. For now, just click **OK** to dismiss the **Flash Accessibility Attributes** dialogue box.

▶ Test your button in your web browser, as before.

User controls

If you have added a video to your website, as explained in Chapter 2, then you will have automatically included user controls. These are the controls which make a video play. If you have added sound to play as a page opens, this is not an example of user controls but if you have experimented with HTML code, or used plug-ins, and added a control to play and stop music, this is another example of a user control being used.

Using specialist script languages

As well as working with Dreamweaver to create interactive elements, you could use elements which have been created in specialist languages, such as JavaScript. If you check the assessment grid for Assessment Objective 4 and the assessment guidance notes, you will see that you are allowed to download elements from the Internet. This would be a great way of adding elements created in some of these specialist script languages. A quick search of the Internet will bring up many sites where you can download a range of interactive elements which you can then use on your website.

Some of the interactive elements you download may require you to work with the HTML view of your website. However, the specifications for this unit accept that when working with scripting you may not always be successful. If this is the case, but you have made a good attempt at making the downloaded feature work, you will be given recognition for your work.

...and finally

The printouts of your website which you provide for assessment at the end of this unit must be annotated to show all interactive elements as well as all hyperlinks. This need not be done on a computer but could simply be a case of going through your printout and marking each of these elements with a pen.

CHAPTER (5)

→ *Assessment Objective 5*

Create a User Form

. . . .

Overview:

In this chapter, you will be shown how to create a user form to collect feedback from users of your site. You will be shown how to add a range of elements, such as drop-down menus, check boxes and radio buttons to make it easier for the user to complete the form. You will then go on to create a user form for your practice assignment.

How this assessment objective will be assessed...

You will be assessed on the following aspects of your user form:

- the complexity of your completed user form
- the method of submission you choose for your user form
- the layout and usability of your user form.

Skills to use...

- You will need to plan and create a user form which collects data from users of your website. This must be well laid out and fit for the purpose.
- The data you collect may be used to help you evaluate your website as part of Assessment Objective 7. Make sure that you ask questions on issues such as how easy the website is to use, whether the website looks good and how easy it is to navigate.

How to achieve...

Pass requirements

P1 You will create a simple form.

P2 The form will use tables to indicate where comments may be added.

P3 Users will be able to print off the form, add comments and send their comments through the post.

P4 The layout of the form may not be appropriate.

Merit requirements

M1 You will create a user form to gather feedback.

M2 Users will be able to complete the form and submit their comments using a submit button.

M3 The form will be mainly well laid out and easy to use.

Using tables to collect data

As we have discussed, a table may be used to organise the layout of a web page. The organisation of text or questions into a logical pattern will improve the layout and usability of a page. Similarly, you could use a table to organise a series of questions which a user can print out and then complete. If you do this, you are basically creating a page which is very much like a word-processed form that you would hand out to people. By hosting the form on the web, anyone can print it out and answer your questions by simply writing on the form with a pen. This form can then be sent through the post to an address you specify – so remember to include an address on the form if you want it to be sent back!

Below is an example of a table you could use to collect information from users of your website. Note that the address has been added at the bottom.

Feedback form

Please use this form to give your opinions on the training you received today.

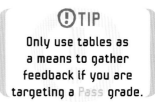

Suitability of accommodation	
Quality of materials and other information you received before the event	
Quality of training you received	
Out of five, with five being the highest, please rate the relevance of today's training to your needs.	

When completed, please print off this form and send it back to 1, The Grove, County Town.

Figure 5.1: *Using a table which can be printed off to gather user feedback.*

This is an acceptable method for gathering information from users. However, remember that if you choose to use this method, you will be limiting yourself to a **Pass** grade for Assessment Objective 5.

We discussed the use of tables in the previous chapter and you should refer back to that section if you are not sure how to set one up.

> **!TIP**
> Only use tables as a means to gather feedback if you are targeting a Pass grade.

What is a user form?

Have you ever been asked to complete an evaluation of a course, or to give written feedback to a class member after a presentation? Both of these are examples of the use of user forms. The user form you create must be an online user form which is included as part of your website and must be used to gather information from users of the website. Because the user form you create will be web based, you will be able to employ a range of extra facilities to make your user form easier to complete. You will also be able to set up your user form so that it can be sent over the Internet, rather than simply handed in or sent through the post.

User form elements

To open the **Forms** toolbar in Dreamweaver, click the down arrow on the left of the toolbar and select **Forms**.

Figure 5.2: *The Forms toolbar.*

There are up to fourteen different choices here but do not worry, you will not be using all of them. The syllabus for Assessment Objective 5 suggests five elements which you may use to collect feedback from a user, either in a table or within a user form. The facilities which are highlighted are sufficient for your needs and so we will concentrate on that list for the rest of this chapter. The facilities we will cover are:

1 text boxes
2 radio buttons and check boxes
3 drop-down menus.

Text boxes

Text boxes are boxes on a form into which the user adds text by selecting the box and typing. If only everything was this easy! There's nothing more to say really, other than to explain the difference between a **text box** and a **text area**.

A **text box** is intended for a short message of maybe only a few words. These words will be on one line only. When you first set up your box on your web page, you will set the size of the box and this cannot be expanded once set. If the user puts in more words than the space allows, the words to the left of the message will disappear from view. They will not cease to exist, but will merely not be shown, unless the user moves back through the message they have just added. This may not worry you but many users will not be aware that they can do this and may see this as a major flaw with the website.

A **text area**, on the other hand, includes a scroll bar. A text area is designed to take data on more than one line and will allow the user to use carriage returns (enter) to end the line. If the user adds more text than you had planned, the vertical scroll bar becomes very obvious; the user is likely to find a text area more user friendly if there is a lot of information to add.

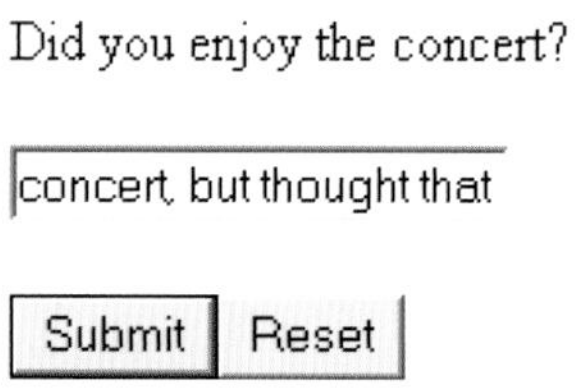

Did you enjoy the concert?

concert, but thought that

Submit | Reset

Figure 5.3: *A text box with some text added.*

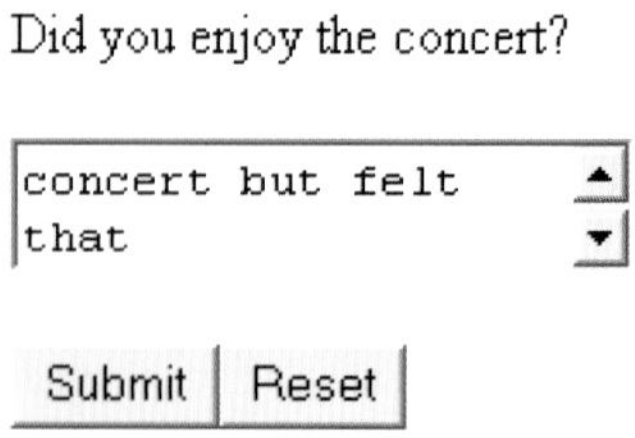

Did you enjoy the concert?

concert but felt
that

Submit | Reset

Figure 5.4: *A text area with text added.*

Radio buttons and check boxes

Radio buttons, like their cousin **check boxes**, allow the user to cast a vote or express an opinion in response to a question. In both cases, the user does this by using the mouse to click on the option for which they wish to vote. The difference between these two elements is that the user can only select one radio button from a group, whereas the user can select more than one check box.

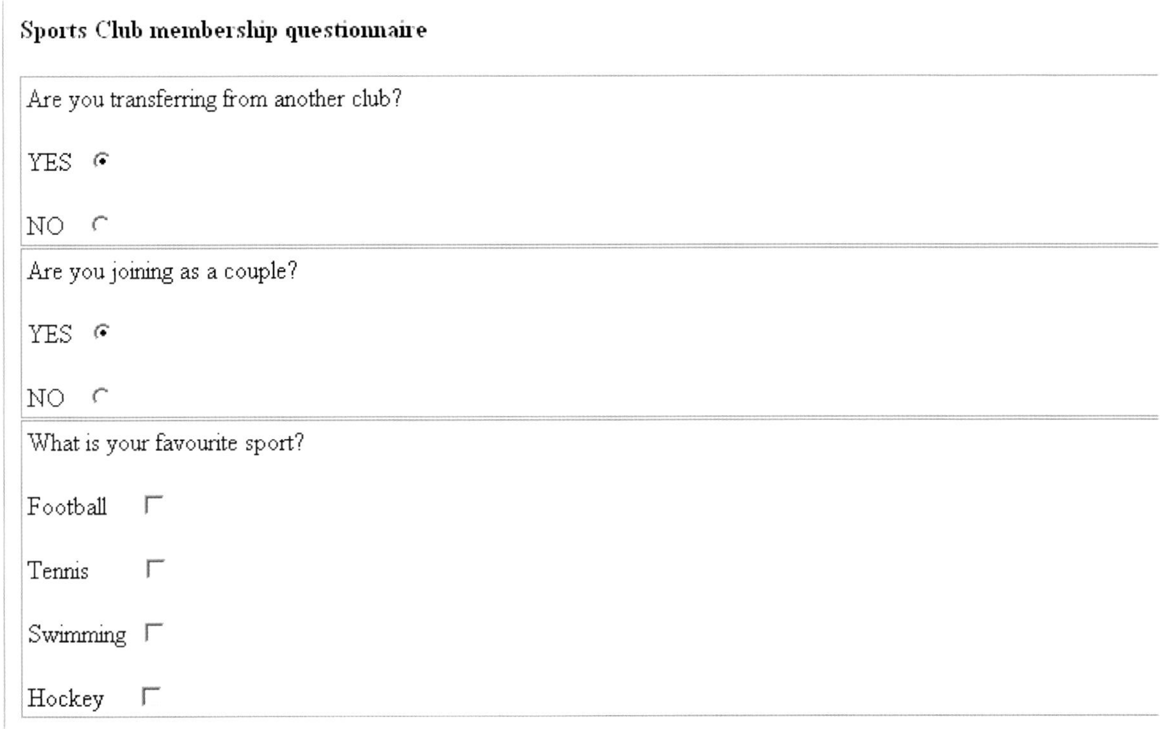

Sports Club membership questionnaire

Are you transferring from another club?

YES   ◉

NO   ○

Are you joining as a couple?

YES   ◉

NO   ○

What is your favourite sport?

Football   ☐

Tennis   ☐

Swimming   ☐

Hockey   ☐

Figure 5.5: *Radio buttons and check boxes used on a form.*

The screenshot above shows how a user form can be used to collect information from a person wishing to join a sports club. The question 'Are you transferring from another club?' can only be answered **yes** or **no**. The user form therefore uses two radio buttons to collect this information. These radio buttons are grouped using the **Radio Group** tool. Because these two radio buttons are grouped, the form can then use another set of radio buttons to collect the answer to 'Are you joining as a couple?'

The third set of questions asks applicants to list their favourite sports. It is perfectly possible that applicants will enjoy more than one sport and so the form uses a set of check boxes to collect this information.

> ⊙**TIP**
>
> Use radio buttons to collect votes when the answers fit the yes/no pattern. Use check boxes where the user is allowed to give more than one answer. If you need to ask more than one yes/no question, use the Radio Group tool to organise radio buttons into groups.

Drop-down menus

The final element you could use is the drop-down menu. Using a drop-down menu adds an element of movement to your work. It is a neat and tidy way of giving options at the point where the user needs to make a decision but it does not obscure elements at other times. As the name suggests, it provides a menu of options in a drop-down list.

Sam's user form

The design for Sam's website shows that she wants a feedback form on the feedback page, which seems like a good place to have it. Sam has provided a design of how she would like the user form to look once completed.

Animal survey

What is your favourite animal?

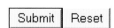

Figure 5.6: *A drop-down menu.*

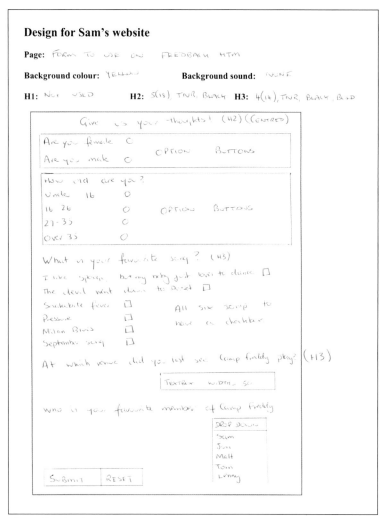

Figure 5.7: *Sam's design.*

How to create Sam's user form

As you can see, Sam wants a user form which combines all of the elements we have just discussed. The activities that follow will show you how to create a user form which would work if properly hosted on a suitable web server. You will use spaces to sort out the layout of this form. However, if you are aiming for a **Distinction** grade, you should use tables, possibly with no visible borders, to improve the layout of the user form.

Creating the form

Follow the steps below to create the form for Sam's website.

Activity 1: Creating a user form...

In this activity you will:

● create a user form.

▶ Open the **feedback** page.

▶ You will be placing the user form just below the **Body Text** on this page. Click at the end of this section and add two empty lines (press **enter** twice) so that there is a gap between the introductory text section and your user form.

▶ Click the **Form** button ▢ on the **Form** toolbar. A red dashed rectangle appears, marking the boundary of the new empty form.

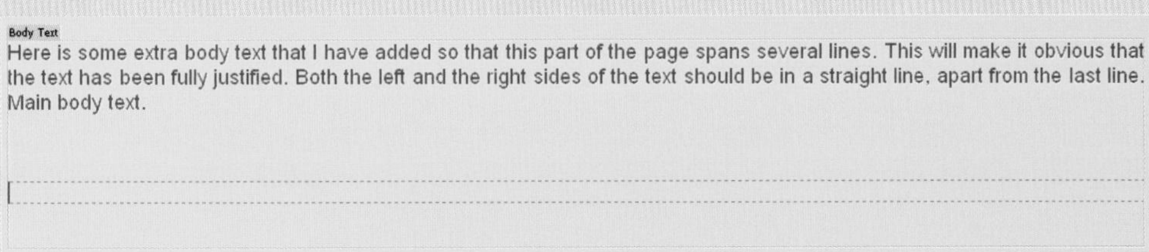

Body Text
Here is some extra body text that I have added so that this part of the page spans several lines. This will make it obvious that the text has been fully justified. Both the left and the right sides of the text should be in a straight line, apart from the last line. Main body text.

Figure 5.8: *The form you have just created.*

Adding the two groups of option buttons

Now you will add option buttons to your form. This activity will use group boxes so that more than one option button may be selected on the form.

Activity 2: Adding two groups of option buttons...

In this activity you will:

● add groups of option buttons to your form.

▶ You now need to add some more content. Your cursor should now be flashing inside the red dashed rectangle. Hit **enter** a few times. You should now see your user form start to expand.

⏵ Click just above the form and add the following text:

Give us your thoughts!

Set the format of this text to **Heading 2**.

You will now add the questions about gender. These will use option buttons to collect their answers. There will be other option buttons on the page, so you must create a group for these first two.

⏵ Click at the top of the form and click **Radio Group** ⊞ on the toolbar. The **Radio Group** dialogue box appears.

⏵ Set the **Name** to **Gender** and set the two labels as shown in Figure 5.9.

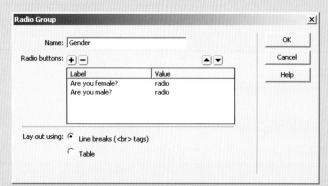

TIP

You can use the plus and minus buttons in the Radio Group dialogue box to change the number of options.

Figure 5.9: *The Radio Group dialogue box.*

⏵ Press **OK** to create the option group.

⏵ You should now click out of this group box. Select below the group box and then hit **enter** once to create a gap and then create a second group box. Use this group box to hold the four questions about age which are shown on Sam's design for her page. Add the text **How old are you?** In the **Heading 3** format.

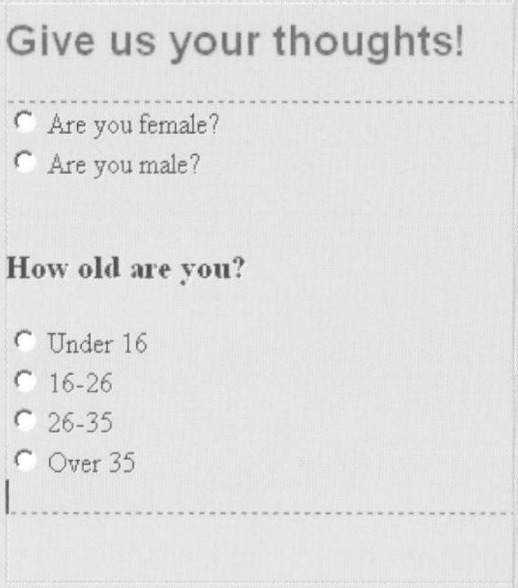

Give us your thoughts!

○ Are you female?
○ Are you male?

How old are you?

○ Under 16
○ 16-26
○ 26-35
○ Over 35

Figure 5.10: *The user form with the gender and age questions added.*

Adding the check boxes

Check boxes are used to capture votes where the answer may require more than one answer to be selected. Check boxes are therefore great at collecting answers from a list where someone has to select more than one option.

Activity 3: Adding check boxes...

In this activity you will:

● add check boxes to your user form.

The design includes a question about favourite songs.

▶ Click in the area below the questions about age.

▶ Type in the sub-title:

What is your favourite song?

▶ This should be in **Heading 3** style.

▶ Hit **enter** to start a new line.

You are now going to add the name of the first song to your web page. The first song listed is the old classic 'I like sponge, but my baby just loves to dance'.

You will now add the check box.

▶ Choose **Checkbox** ☑ from the toolbar.

▶ Add the song's title as the **Label** in the dialogue box that appears and click **OK**.

▶ Repeat this process for the other five songs:

● The devil went down to Dorset
● Snakebite fever
● Pressure
● Milan blues
● September song

Adding the text box

You will need a text box to collect the answer to the next question. This question will be below the six song options.

Activity 4: Adding a text box...

In this activity you will:

● add a text box to your user form.

▶ Select the area below the section about favourite songs.

▶ Type in the question:

At which venue did you last see Camp Freddy play?

▶ This should be in **Heading 3** format.

▶ Choose **Text Field** ⌨ from the toolbar and click **OK** without adding a **Label**.

Change the settings for a form field

So far, we have accepted all of the setting decisions which Dreamweaver has given us. However, the size of the text box is too small, so we need to increase the amount of characters which it will show at once.

Activity 5: Change the settings for a form field...

In this activity you will:

● change the settings for a form field on your user form.

▶ Click on the text box you have just added.

▶ In the **Properties** panel, set **Char width** to **50** and press **enter**.

You should see that your text box has become wider.

Adding the drop-down list

Now you need to add the **drop-down** list. This will be a list of each of the five members of the group.

Activity 6: Adding a drop-down list...

In this activity you will:

● add a drop-down list to your user form.

▶ Select the area below the text box. Type in the question:

Who is your favourite member of Camp Freddy?

▶ This should be in **Heading 3** format.

▶ Choose **List/Menu** 📄 from the toolbar.

▶ Click **OK** to dismiss the **Input Tag Accessibility Attributes** dialogue box.

▶ Click the **List Values** button in the **Properties** pane. The **List Values** dialogue box will appear.

▶ Enter five entries – one for each member of the band (Sam, Jon, Matt, Tom and Lenny). Use the name for both the **Item Label** and **Value** in each case.

▶ Press **OK** when you have finished.

Adding a button

The final element you need to add is the submit button.

Activity 7: Adding a button...

In this activity you will:

● add a submit button to your user form.

▶ Select the area below the drop-down list.

▶ Choose **Button** ▢ from the toolbar.

▶ Click **OK** to dismiss the **Input Tag Accessibility Attributes** dialogue box.

A button named **Submit** should appear on your form.

Proof that your form would work

The specifications for this unit state that for a **Distinction** level in Assessment Objective 5, you must create a form which is:

Well laid out, easy to use and will work.

You may be wondering how you could show that this would work. You are not expected to publish your website to the web. However, if you can show that your website would be sent to the correct email address, if your site were published, this would be sufficient evidence that your form meets this requirement.

Activity 8: Proving that a form would work...

In this activity you will:

● provide evidence that your user form would work.

▶ Click the **<form#form1>** tag on the horizontal bar at the bottom of the main part of the Dreamweaver window, just above the **Properties** pane. This will select the form.

▶ In the **Properties** pane, set the **Action** to **mailto:** followed by your email address.

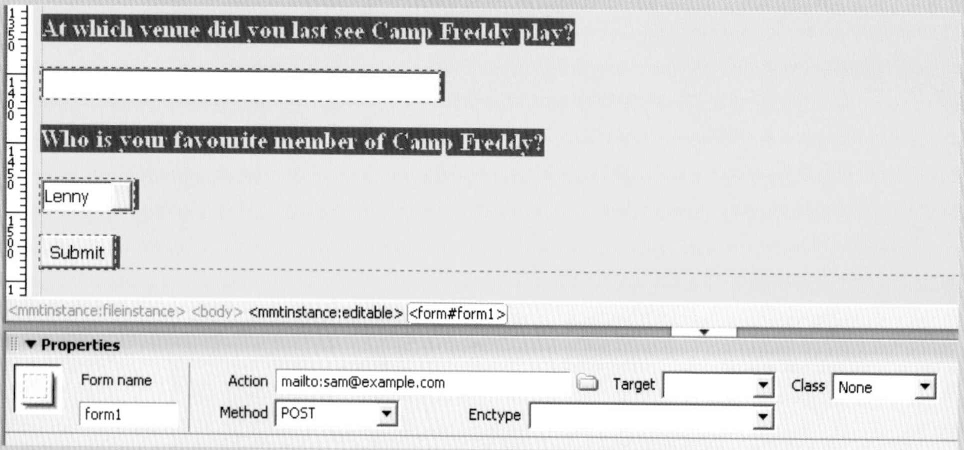

Figure 5.11: *Setting a destination for the form.*

▶ For evidence, create a screenshot of this page.

▶ Your form is now complete and fully functional. Well done!

...and finally

If you have worked through this practice assignment from the very beginning, you should now have a web page which works well and looks great! However, you may notice that there are a few places where you still have the words **main body text**. This is your opportunity to make your website look a little bit different from all the others created by students who have also worked through this book.

Activity 9: Adding that touch of individual flair...

In this activity you will:

● add a touch of individuality to your website.

▶ Select the area on your web page which says **Body Text**.

▶ Add your own text to the page.

CHAPTER 6
→ *Assessment Objective 6*
Test Your Website

Overview:

This chapter will explain the reasons for testing. You will then be given some examples of how a website may be tested. You will then test the website you have created for Sam and make any improvements necessary so that your completed website works as intended.

How this assessment objective will be assessed...

You will be assessed on the following aspects of your testing:

* the amount of testing you do
* what you choose to test and how you choose to do that testing
* how you follow up any issues that your testing uncovers
* the evidence you provide to show that you have carried out the testing and made changes as necessary.

Skills to use...

* You will need to work in a very organised manner.
* Your testing must be planned and must cover all the main areas of the website.
* The testing you choose to do must be appropriate, so you will need to have a sound understanding of *why* you are testing before you start to carry out your tests.
* To achieve the higher grades, you must produce screenshots or annotated HTML code to prove that you have made changes to your website.

How to achieve...

Pass requirements

P1 You will test your website with at least four tests. These tests must include all hyperlinks and images.

P2 Most of these tests will be appropriate.

P3 You must submit all five pages as evidence of testing.

Merit requirements

M1 You will test your website with at least five tests. These tests must include all hyper-links and images.

M2 The tests will cover most of the main areas of the website.

M3 The tests will be appropriate.

M4 There will be annotated HTML code or screenshots providing evidence of before and after changes where appropriate.

M5 You must submit all five pages as evidence of testing.

Distinction requirements

D1 You will test your website with at least six tests. These tests must include all hyper-links and images.

D2 The tests will cover all main areas of the website.

D3 The tests will be appropriate.

D4 The test table will include an indication of any action needed to solve any problems discovered.

D5 There will be annotated HTML code or screenshots providing evidence of before and after changes where appropriate.

D6 You must submit all five pages as evidence of testing.

What is testing?

Testing is the process of making sure that what you *think* you have done actually *has been* done. Before you finish your website, you must test all aspects to ensure that your website works as intended. There are three main tasks you should perform:

- testing all links
- checking the layout and alignment of all elements
- proof-reading text.

Why test?

Testing is an example of best practice. This means that if you want to be considered a good web designer, you must test that your website works as intended. If you do not test your website, you might be lucky and not have any problems. However, it is far more likely that you will have made some mistakes in your work. Well-planned testing will find these mistakes and let you correct them before the client or anyone else looks at the website you have created. The best way to ensure that you test all of the main elements of your website is to create a **test table**. This is basically a list of all the elements in your website and how each of them may be tested. A good test table will test every aspect of the website and let you fix any problems before the completed website is passed to the client for their final checks.

Key terms

Test table

A table showing which elements of a website will be tested and how.

Testing a website

There are six main tests which you can apply to websites.

1 Do all of the elements I placed on my website appear when the page is opened in a web browser?

2 Do all of these elements appear *where* I want them to on the web page?

3 Do all of these elements appear *how* I want them to?

4 Do my hyperlinks work?

5 Have I made any spelling mistakes?

6 Does what I have written make sense?

Some of you will have used a cascading style sheet to set up your web pages. This will also need to be tested. There is a final section at the end of the discussion of the six tests which explains how to test a cascading style sheet (see page 90).

Do all of the elements appear?

This is a simple test but also an important one. If you have spent a lot of time creating a website, and have made painful decisions about what is an appropriate image and what is not, it would seem silly to risk having your most important image not appear. The simplest way to test whether all elements of your website appear is to use the **Preview in Browser** facility. This is an option on the **File** menu. You should use this to choose which of the browsers installed on your machine you will use to view the website.

Do all the elements appear *where* I want them to?

It is very easy to have something appear in the wrong position, especially if you build your website piece by piece. When you add a new element, it can change where other elements appear.

Similarly, tables can cause problems, especially more complicated ones. When you create extra rows or columns in a table, elements you have already added can be pushed to the side or down. This may not be what you intended.

Luckily, testing that every element appears where it should is as simple as looking at each page and comparing what you see with your design plans. This can be done either using the **Design** view or by using the **Preview in Browser** function.

Do all of the elements appear *how* I want them to?

This is the test where you check that what you had planned to be a special heading, or even body text, actually appears as a special heading or as body text. There are two ways to check this. The first is to check it visually, which means looking at the page preview in your browser. The second check is to watch the contents of the **Properties** pane as you move through your page in **Design** view. As the properties change, are the rules you thought you had applied actually being applied?

Do my hyperlinks work?

In order to test every hyperlink on your website, you need to be organised. It can be easy to miss some links on a large website which has a lot of them. The easiest way to make sure you check every link is to create a list of all the hyperlinks as you create them. When you have completed your website, you then have a list of all the hyperlinks you have used. You can then just add your list to the test table.

This may seem like cheating, as testing is done when a website is finished but, as you know that you will need to carry out testing, the best plan is to be ready. Testing hyperlinks is as simple as clicking on them in the browser preview and seeing where you are taken.

When checking hyperlinks, you should also test any rollovers you have used. These should work as planned. It is very easy to use the wrong rollover image, or to set a rollover to work on a mouse click when you wanted the rollover to work on a mouse-over.

As well as testing hyperlinks and whether they work, you should also check the general navigation against your original plan. There are two things you need to test here:

1 Can all web pages in the website be accessed?
2 Have you followed the plan and have all the hyperlinks you meant to include actually been set up?

Have I made any spelling mistakes?

There are two ways to check for any spelling errors on your website. The first is to use the spell check facility while in **Design** view. You start a spell check by selecting **Text...Check Spelling** from the menu. This will highlight most spelling errors and suggest corrections. This facility operates in exactly the same way as any other spell checker so you should already be confident about how to accept or dismiss suggested corrections.

The second way to test that you have not made any spelling mistakes is to read through your work. This is not as easy as it sounds (see below)!

Does what I have written make sense?

As well as letting you check for spelling mistakes, reading through your work helps you to check that your writing makes sense. However, when reading through your own work, it is easy to read what you *think* is there and not what is *actually* there. This is because you remember what you have written and also because you know what you were trying to say.

There are a few tricks you can use to help you proof-read your own work:

- Do not read your work as soon as you have finished it. If you leave a gap of a few days, you are far more likely to look at it with fresh eyes.
- Read the work. This may sound obvious, but this means read *every word*, not just scan-read the work. This will help you pick up words which you have spelt incorrectly and areas where your writing is not clear.
- Do not interpret your work. There is a simple rule: if you do not understand what you have written, nobody else will. Write the section again.

Testing a cascading style sheet

This is a separate section for those of you who have used cascading style sheets. The great thing about a cascading style sheet is that it defines the style in any page to which it is applied. This includes the page when it is in **Design** view. So, as you move through your page in **Design** view, you should see that those elements which you think are set by the cascading style sheet do actually follow the cascading style sheet rules. If they do not, then the cascading style sheet has not been applied properly or has maybe even been missed off.

A second way to test whether a cascading style sheet has been applied correctly is to change the settings within the cascading style sheet. These changes should then be applied to any web pages which are controlled by the cascading style sheet. Obviously, once you are sure that the cascading style sheet is properly set up, you should change the cascading style sheet settings back to those which fit the needs of the brief.

Creating a test table

You must use a test table to plan and show the results of your testing. A test table has five features:

- what you are testing
- how you are testing it
- what you expect to happen
- what actually happened
- what action you took to solve the problem.

The first three features are all part of planning. The last two show the results.

Part of a test table is shown below; the focus here is on the hyperlinks. You know that for hyperlinks there is one main test, but this website uses rollovers on the main link on the page and so this has been tested as well.

What is being tested?	How is this element tested?	Expected outcome	Actual outcome	Action taken
Hyperlink from index.htm to friends.htm	Click on the hyperlink	Friends.htm opens	Friends. htm opened	None required
Hyperlink from index.htm to pictures.htm	Click on the hyperlink	Pictures.htm opens	Friends. htm opened	I deleted the link and replaced it with the correct link to pictures. htm. I checked the new link and it worked.
Hyperlink from index.htm to pictures.htm (rollover effect)	Click on the hyperlink	Linked images changes to pictures.jpg	Picture changes as planned	None required

How do I prove that I have carried out testing?

Evidence is always a problem but the only real evidence that you need to show to prove that you have carried out testing is a completed test table. However, for **Merit** and **Distinction**, you also need to make some changes to your website as a result of the testing and provide before and after screenshots of the improvements you have made. For a **Distinction** grade, you must also include a written description of what you need to fix.

Activity 1: Testing...

In this activity you will:

● check your understanding of the evidence required to prove that you have tested your website.

Look at the test table opposite. This is part of a test table for a website.

▶ What extra tests would you need to add to the tests shown in the test table to be awarded a Pass?

▶ As well as the extra tests you described above, what extra evidence do you need to provide to be awarded a **Merit**?

▶ What extra piece of evidence moves a **Merit** grade piece of work onto a **Distinction** grade?

Testing Sam's website

We have discussed the types of test you could use. Now is the time to discuss how you will test the website you have created for Sam. We will list the elements which need testing. You will then construct the test table and carry out the testing.

These are the elements on Sam's website:

● hyperlinks
● images
● tables
● a form
● text
● headings
● background colour
● animation
● video
● sound.

Each of these elements needs to be tested. Some elements will need more than one test. Text, for example, will need to be checked to see that you have used the correct font style, colour and size. A large test table can become very complicated, so create a different test table for each web page. Once you have created the first one, you will be able to use it as a template for the others, because it will include common elements, such as introductory text.

Activity 2: Creating a test table...

In this activity you will:

● create a test table for the **index** page on Sam's website.

▶ Using appropriate software, create a table with the same headings as on the test table on page 90. You are going to start by listing the hyperlinks on this page. In the left-hand column, list the four hyperlinks on this page. You should call them by their target page (i.e. **link to the members page**).

▶ In the second column, explain how each link will be tested. For each of these links, the test will be to click on them.

▶ The third column will be used to show the expected result. The expected result for each of these tests is that the correct page will open. When you create the table, your expected action should include the name of the page.

You will not complete the remaining columns until you do the testing.

▶ Continue to list the elements on the page which you will test, how you will test them and the expected result.

▶ Once you have completed the test table, save your sheet and create further test tables for the remaining web pages in Sam's website.

You have now created the test table for Sam's website.

Activity 3: Test Sam's website...

In this activity you will:

● complete the tests you have listed in the test plan.

▶ Use the tests you have included on your test table to test Sam's website. Use the result column to record what happened when you did the test. Use the action required column to make a note of what you need to do if you find any errors.

▶ Provide screenshots of the web pages you have created to show the errors which you find. Make the necessary changes and then provide screenshots of the web pages after you have made the changes.

> ⊙TIP
>
> You can use Site...Check Links Sitewide to check that all of the hyperlinks you have added do actually lead to pages that exist. This doesn't prove that the links lead to the correct pages, but is a useful additional check, particularly for links to external websites. Site...Reports also provides some checks that you might wish to run.

What happens if I do not find any errors?

This is unlikely but it could happen. The specifications say that you should respond to any issues by making necessary changes. If there are no errors, no changes are necessary. Your completed test table will be evidence that you have carried out testing and have found no errors with your work.

> ⊙TIP
>
> These tests are appropriate for Sam's website. They may not be appropriate for the website you develop. Remember to make your own test table with relevant tests. As well as your test table, you must submit a printout of all five web pages.

CHAPTER 7

→ Assessment Objective 7

Evaluate Your Website

Overview:

In this chapter, we will discuss how you should evaluate the website you produce. This will be presented as a series of issues which you could consider. This chapter will not be based on the website you produced for Sam.

How this assessment objective will be assessed...

You will be assessed on the following aspects of your evaluation:

- the amount of detail you include in your evaluation
- how accurately you assess your own strengths and weaknesses.

Skills to use...

You will need to identify the purpose and audience for your website. This is information you should have had when you first started to create your website. You will then need to assess how well your website meets this purpose and meets the needs of the target audience.

You will also need to be able to assess the readability, usability and accessibility of your website. We will discuss these in the main section of this chapter. You will not be expected to make the changes which your report identifies, merely to know that, if the changes were made, they would improve the quality of your website.

Your final task is to comment on the strengths and weaknesses of your work. You will need to be very clear what you have done and whether you could do it better if you had to do the work again. You should also comment on your working practices.

How to achieve...

Pass requirements

P1   You will produce a brief evaluation of your work.

P2   The evaluation will cover:
- o   the suitability of the website for purpose
- o   the suitability of the website for audience
- o   the readability of the website.

All comments in the evaluation will be supported by examples from the website.

P3   You will give limited examples of your own strengths and weaknesses.

Merit requirements

M1 You will produce a detailed evaluation of your work.

M2 The evaluation will cover:
- o the suitability of the website for purpose
- o the suitability of the website for audience
- o the readability of the website
- o the usability of the website.

All comments in the evaluation will be supported by examples from the website.

M3 You will give detailed examples of your own strengths and weaknesses.

Distinction requirements

D1 You will produce an extensive evaluation of your work.

D2 The evaluation will cover:
- o the suitability of the website for purpose
- o the suitability of the website for audience
- o the readability of the website
- o the usability of the website
- o the accessibility of the website.

All comments in the evaluation will be supported by examples from the website.

D3 You will give thorough examples of your own strengths and weaknesses.

Evaluation

When you have finished your website, your final task will be to evaluate your own work. This will cover two areas:

- the quality of the website
- the strengths and weaknesses of your working practice.

Assessing the quality of your website

There are five areas in which you can assess your website:

1 suitability for purpose and audience
2 content
3 readability
4 usability
5 accessibility.

We will now discuss each of these areas in turn.

Suitability for purpose and audience

There are two areas to think about here. If something is suitable for purpose, then it does the job it was intended to do. For example, the clothes you wear during the summer are, hopefully, able to cope with the range of heat and rain which you may encounter. These clothes are therefore suitable for purpose. However, the same clothes would not protect you from the weather in the winter. If you wore them then, your clothes would not be suitable for purpose.

Similarly, your website will have a set purpose. We discussed the possible purposes of a website in Chapter 1 and you should have included some comment about the purpose of your website in your initial planning. When you come to the end of your work on the website, you need to look at your work and decide, truthfully, whether your work does indeed do what the client has asked for. If your client wants a website to generate sales, will your website do this? If your client wants a website to share information, will your website do this? It is perfectly possible that you may have created a website which will not perform as intended, and yet your analysis can still be awarded good marks if you understand that this is the case.

The second thing to think about is suitability for the target audience. We also discussed target audience in Chapter 1 and it is a concept that you should have come across in other ICT lessons. The specifications for this unit allow you to decide who the target audience is for your website but that does not mean you can make up an inappropriate or silly target audience; your target audience must fit the task your client gave you.

You will be able to get a better feel for suitability for purpose and audience as you discuss the issues covered below: content, readability, usability and accessibility.

Content

What have you included in your website? Have you chosen to include a lot of material which is irrelevant? Maybe you have chosen to include only a few elements and now you realise you should have added more. When you consider content, you are really thinking about the range of elements you have used, including images. All should suit the purpose and the target audience.

Readability

This refers to how easy it is to read your web pages. If you have chosen a font which is difficult to read or a font size which is too small, these choices may make your web pages difficult to read. Similarly, if you have chosen a font colour which does not stand out against your background, this will cause problems. This is a particular problem if you have chosen an image as a background. If you have used an image which is a mix of colours, it is very likely that any text you have placed on the page will be difficult to read.

Finally in this section, think about the language you have chosen to use. This does not mean have you written your website in Welsh or German; both of these choices would be fine if that was what the brief required. Language here means the words you have used. As you have read this book you have, hopefully, been able to understand the points which have been made. This is because the language in this book has been carefully chosen so that it is **accessible** to the target audience, which is you. This is the choice of words and the expressions which have been used. Short sentences make points easier to understand. If you have used short sentences, your work should also be easy to understand.

Usability

You must consider how easy your website is to use. This includes the **navigation** you have used. As you review your website, ask yourself whether you could get back to the homepage easily, or whether you could find a section you wanted. If you would find it difficult, most users would find it impossible.

When thinking about hyperlinks and usability, there are two main issues. The first is consistency and the second is the type of hyperlink you use.

If you have not used the same style or type of hyperlink throughout your work, the user will find it difficult to realise where the links are on a page. It is a good idea to use a consistent style of link and to place your links in the same place. This will allow the user to find links where they expect them to be and so feel more confident in using your website. People generally feel more comfortable when they feel they know their environment, and websites are no different.

Think about the style of link you use. What might start off as a good idea may become a bad one if overused. Look at the section of a website below:

The answers to this question can be found <u>here</u>. However, Martin's view can be found <u>here</u> and <u>here</u>. A better answer is <u>here</u>, but if you want it in French, it is <u>here</u>. <u>Here</u> is a picture which shows him as a young man and again <u>here</u>.

The web author has used the word **here** as a textual link seven times in four sentences. This makes it very difficult for the reader to decide which links to follow. Imagine if this were a whole paragraph. The user would be faced with a massive amount of links with no real idea of what was happening. If your website had used similar navigation, you would probably decide that it was not very usable.

This can also be true of buttons. If you have used a **home button**, is it easy to identify?

Just like the example of too many text links all using 'here', if you use too many buttons on a page, the user may not be able to find the button they want and so will not be able to navigate the website easily.

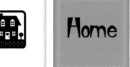

Figure 7.1: *Which is the home button?*

Finally in this section, think about any navigation bars you have used. A navigation bar on every page can make a website very easy to use but only if it is a simple navigation bar without too many links. If you include too many links, your navigation bar will become overcomplicated and difficult to use.

Accessibility

You must consider how accessible your website is for all users. Some users may wish to use a **reader**. For those readers who are visually impaired, this can be a very useful tool, as it reads the page out. However, readers cannot cope with images as the HTML code merely says where the image is and does not describe the image. However, **alternative text** can be added to an image and read by a reader. If you have not used alternative text, your work will not be as accessible as it would be if you had.

Alternative text can be added to an image by selecting it and editing the **Alt** attribute in the **Properties** pane.

> ⊘ **TIP**
> You could use Site…Reports to run the Accessibility report, as proof that your site is accessible.

Key terms

Readers

Software which reads the HTML code for a web page and, using speech synthesiser software, reads the page to the user.

Alternative text

Text which describes an image – this can be added by editing the **Alt** property of an image.

Assessing strengths and weaknesses

The final part of your evaluation must be an assessment of your strengths and weaknesses. Here are some areas you could consider.

- **Planning.** Think about how well you planned your work. Did your final website fit this plan, or did you move away from the plan to some extent?
- **Creation of the website.** In this section, you could discuss your knowledge of the software and whether this affected your work.

...and finally

The specifications stress that you are evaluating but not necessarily improving. For example, if you decide that the font you used was a mistake, then you can say so, but you are not required to make any changes to your website. Evaluation happens very much at the end when you have finished working on the website and 'finished' means you have stopped, so you do not need to go back and make changes.

UNIT (20)

Creating Animation for the WWW Using ICT

In this unit you will cover the following...

A01 A discussion about how to review animations, helping you to gather some ideas about which elements to include in your own work

A02 A review of different methods you can use to plan animations

A03 Creating your sample animation

A04 Testing your animation

Introduction to Unit 20

This unit is one of the half units which you can combine with full units to gain full qualifications in this course. Animation is a skill which you may use in web design or multimedia and so the work you produce for this unit could be used to enhance the work you complete for other units.

This unit will concentrate on the use of Macromedia Flash software. Flash is a very flexible piece of software which uses a range of tools and facilities to produce animations ranging from quite simple buttons through to whole websites. You will work through a sample project which will allow you to practise working with Flash. At the end of every section there are further ideas or extension tasks which you could look at to widen your understanding of what Flash can do.

CHAPTER

→ *Assessment Objective 1*

Review Several Existing Animations

Overview:

In this unit, you will be producing an animation for use on a website. Before you do, you will need to review several existing animations. These animations may be ones which you have found yourself, by looking on the Internet, or may be provided for you by your centre. If you are looking on the Internet, any of the following could be considered:

* animated gifs
* Flash or Shockwave movies
* animated web banners.

Your review of each animation should cover the following:

* the good and not so good features
* the aim of the animation
* how the aims of the animation are met
* if the aims are not met, an explanation of why
* possible improvements to the animations.

A worksheet to help you review animations is available in the Unit 20 Resources zip file which can be downloaded from the OCR Nationals in ICT (Units 2 & 20) Student Resources page on the Payne Gallway website: www.payne-gallway.co.uk

How this assessment objective will be assessed...

Assessment Objective 1 will be assessed by the amount of detail you include in your review of each animation. As a minimum, you must list the good and not so good features of an animation. However, if you add more detail to your review, such as identifying the aim of the animation, and then go on to suggest improvements, you will achieve a higher grade.

Skills to use...

The ability to identify the aim of an animation is a key skill here. If you are clear about how to do this, you will then find it far easier to criticise an animation. We will discuss tricks for identifying the aim of an animation below. You must also be able to make valid criticisms. When you come to criticise the animations, be aware that the first thing which comes into your head is not necessarily the most relevant criticism.

How to achieve...

Pass requirements

P1 You will list the good and not so good features of at least two different animations.

Merit requirements

M1 You will identify the aim of each animation you are reviewing.

M2 You will give a detailed explanation of the good and not so good features of at least two different animations.

M3 You will suggest possible improvements which could be made to each animation.

Distinction requirements

D1 You will identify the aim of each animation you are reviewing.

D2 You will give a thorough explanation of the good and not so good features of at least two different animations.

D3 You will suggest a range of valid improvements which would help each animation meet its aims.

What is an animation?

In general terms, animation could be defined as breathing life into an object. When applied to working with computer software, this definition still applies. Computer animation is the process of taking a number of objects and joining them together in a way which makes them look as if the object is moving.

There are many different types of animation, not all of which are computer based. You may have created animations of your own by creating a flip book animation. This is where you draw a series of slightly different images on the pages of a book and, as you flip through the pages, so the slight changes blur into each other to create the illusion of movement. This form of animation represents **frame based** animation. This is by far the oldest form of animation and was the technique used by the earliest cartoons up to relatively recently. The other form of animation has come about as animation software has become more powerful. This form of animation allows the author to set an object at a start point and an end point and then uses the tools within the software to create the illusion of movement. This has greatly reduced the amount of effort required to produce even the most simple of animations. This technique is called **tweening**, which is short for **in betweening.**

There are software packages which allow you to work with both methods. Software such as Jasc Animation Shop can be used to create frame-by-frame animations. Alternatively, software such as Macromedia Flash allows you to create animations which use **tweening** to create the illusion of movement between two fixed points. You can also use Macromedia Flash to create frame-by-frame animation, but it is probably better known as an example of tweening software.

Key terms

Frame based animation

Animation created by drawing each frame of a presentation. Each frame differs from the next only slightly, so that as the frames are shown one after another, the changes create the illusion of movement.

Tweening

This is short for 'in betweening'. Tweening is the process of filling in movement between two fixed points.

Tween based animation

Animation based on the use of tweening to create the illusion of movement.

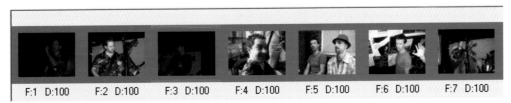

F:1 D:100   F:2 D:100   F:3 D:100   F:4 D:100   F:5 D:100   F:6 D:100   F:7 D:100

Figure 8.1: *Frames in a frame-by-frame animation (Animation Pro).*

Choosing an animation to review

This may be your choice or you may be given an animation by your centre. The first thing to stress is that, however you make your choice of which animations to review, you must review two different animations.

The second issue to stress is that you do not need to spend a great deal of time finding the coolest animation which will impress your friends. The reason why you are doing this task is to show that you know what makes a good animation and also so that you may get some design hints from the animations you review.

Identify the aims of an animation

This is not as difficult as you may think. The aim of an animation is simply what it is trying to do. Animations, like websites, have set aims. Below is a short list of possible aims of an animation:

- to add or increase interest
- to entertain
- to inform.

There are many different aims of an animation which all fit into the first, general aim. For example:

'I have included animation to attract customers to my website. This helps me to sell more.'

'People reported that my website was dull. I added some animation to jazz things up.'

Both of these aims are trying to add or increase interest to a website.

Entertainment should be the easiest of all to identify. However, what sometimes looks like entertainment is actually an attempt to sell something. If the animation you are looking at is on a commercial site which is trying to sell a product, then the purpose of the animation is probably to increase interest, so that more customers will visit the site. However, if the animation is on a site which gives examples of animations or is clearly an animation site, then the purpose is probably to entertain.

The final purpose is to inform. There are many reasons why people may choose to use animation rather than real-life characters to inform. These range from a belief that a cartoon character may be a strong image which will stick in people's minds through to the fact that dangerous situations are better drawn than acted out for real. Examples of the latter would be warning about the danger of crossing the road without looking, or putting to sea without telling the coastguard. Whatever the reason for choosing animation to deliver the message, there is a clear difference between using animation to inform and using animation to increase interest. The first one is done so that people learn from the message, the second is intended to attract potential viewers.

Identify the good and not so good features

There are a number of skills you will need to develop if you wish to identify the good and bad points of an animation. You need to be able to:

* identify any target audience for an animation
* decide on the impact of different features
* recognise when features have been badly or inaccurately constructed or animated.

Identifying the target audience

The concept of a target audience was discussed on page 6. If you wish to review this concept, you should refer back to this chapter now.

Deciding on the impact of features

Animation can have many features. These include:

* the images, graphics or video used
* the sound used
* any buttons or navigation
* the animation itself.

Any animation will have some, most or all of the features listed above. As you review the animation you are studying, consider each in turn and decide how effective it is. The table below lists some common areas you could discuss for each of these key features.

TIP

You may need to differentiate between photographs and what may be called drawn pictures. We will use the term images to refer to photographs and graphics to refer to images which have been created on a computer.

Feature	Possible concerns
Images	• size
	• resolution
	• content
	• relevance
	• effect on the viewer
Graphics	• size
	• resolution
	• content
	• relevance
	• accuracy
	• the extent to which they are lifelike
	• effect on the viewer
Video	• size
	• content
	• relevance
	• length
	• quality of filming
	• effect on the viewer
Sound	• content
	• clarity
	• relevance
	• length
	• overall quality of recording
	• effect on the listener
Buttons or navigation	• how much they stand out on a page
	• clarity of purpose
	• size
Animation	• accuracy of movement
	• type of movement
	• choice of effects
	• speed of animation

You may be able to think of further issues as you review animations.

Recognising badly constructed or animated features

Just how do you recognise badly constructed or animated features? This has already been mentioned in the section above, but this question needs to be looked at more closely. As we have already said, animation is the process of creating the illusion of movement. It is possible to create the illusion of movement in objects which would not normally move. In the next chapter, you will look at creating an animation working with a ball. A ball is, pretty much, a ball and it would be quite difficult to get it wrong.

However, how good are you at drawing real-life objects? Some people can make a box and a bit of shading look like a car speeding down the motorway or like a bird in flight. However, other people find it difficult to draw even stick men. When you review animations, think about what the author or artist is trying to do. If the animation uses basic shape to good effect, then it's a success, but if the animation tries to use basic shapes to recreate real life and fails, despite trying, the feature is not as good as it should be.

Figure 8.2: *Which image is the more lifelike?*

Animation can also be judged by how well it moves the objects. For example, it is complicated to create an animation which shows walking. Not only is it difficult to remove the stiffness from the animated characters on the screen but creating the correct walking pace is also difficult, especially as just about everybody knows how fast people walk. Science fiction monsters are far easier to do, they can move as stiffly or as slowly as you like!

Other problems may arise because the animator has animated a few characters on the screen and then used these characters more than once. Examples of this may be seen in films which have used animated battle scenes to create the illusion of thousands of troops. As you watch these scenes, it sometimes occurs to you that every horse is moving the same way every few seconds, or that the archer in the red tunic keeps shooting the same arrow. These are both examples of poor animation.

Commenting on good and not so good features

If you are aiming for a **Pass** grade, you will only need to list the features of at least two animations. However, for higher grades, you will need to give some further explanation of the features you are identifying. For a **Merit** grade, you must give a detailed explanation and for a **Distinction**, you must give a thorough explanation. The table below shows some examples of how you could comment on features you have found. The animation which is being reviewed here is a short piece which has a spoken introduction which is followed by a car chase. The animation has been used on a children's website.

Feature	Comment
Sound	**Good:** I liked the pace of the music which played throughout the animation. It created a feeling of tension in the animation which went with the aim. The spoken introduction was a clever idea because it set the scene well by using words which young children could understand. **Bad:** The sound quality was very poor. I think that it was very badly recorded, as there was a background hiss and crackle all through the music. This was also true of the spoken part but it was not so bad.
Quality of animation	**Good:** The animation looked like a cartoon of real life with some good graphics used. During the car chase, the movement across the screen was very smooth and the part where the yellow car speeded up was really well done. **Bad:** I thought some of the movement of people was a bit stiff and maybe the people moved too quickly. The explosion after the crash was very bad as the boom animation just did not work properly.

⊘TIP

Due to the amount of detail included here, this candidate would probably be awarded a Merit mark. However, if they went on to add more detail for other features of this animation, the student might be awarded a Distinction. For example, the comment about the boom animation is extremely vague and would benefit from an explanation of what this animation was trying to do and what more would be needed to make this animation effective.

Assessing whether the aims have been met

Once you have identified the aims of an animation, you should be able to assess whether these have been met. This assessment may be based on your own judgement of the animation as well as the good and not so good features which it includes.

The decision about whether the aims have been met is, to some extent, based on the impression you have drawn of the animation. The evidence you have gathered will be the list of good and not so good features. If you find that there are many features which are not so good, it is likely that the aims of the animation will not have been met. The opposite is also true; if you find that the animation is generally good, with elements and animations which suit the target audience, the aims of the animation are likely to have been met.

Suggesting improvements

The key issue here is relevance. Suggesting a long list of clever tricks which would not suit the aims or the target audience will not earn you any marks. Try to keep your suggestions relevant to the task.

You should also try to provide a range of suggestions. One technique you could use to ensure that you include a range of suggestions on how to improve the animation, is to list each type of element and make a comment in general terms, which you then back up with examples.

Below is a selection from a table reviewing an animation aimed at adding movement to a website about cycling.

Element	Comment	Suggested improvement
Graphics	The original graphics seemed to have been very small and by the end of the motion tween, during which the graphics grew to about twice their original size, all graphics were very pixellated.	The original graphics should have been larger so that they did not pixellate as they became bigger on the screen.
	Some of the graphics did not seem appropriate. The animation was about cycling, but some graphics were more relevant to motorcycling. The second graphic which appeared showed a motorcyclist enjoying the view from the top of a steep hill.	Graphics need to be chosen with thought to the target audience and the purpose of the animation. The graphic of the motorcycle is inappropriate and should be changed for an image of a cyclist.
Animations	When the ball motion tweened from left to right and then back again, the ball did not quite go all the way back and so when the animation started again, the ball jumped to the start of the animation.	The animation should have been tested to check that the ball went back to the correct starting point. Because the ball went back to the start of the line, the software rulers or the on screen guides should have been used to fix the ball in the correct place at the end of the animation.

> ⊙TIP
>
> This is not a complete review of the animation but if this candidate continued to review the animation in such detail, they would probably be awarded a Distinction.

The comments in this table are clearly relevant and cover a range of issues. By highlighting each aspect of the animation, the candidate has made sure that she covers this task in good detail.

CHAPTER 9
→ *Assessment Objective 2*

Design an Animation

Overview:

Planning is a vital task when producing an animation. If you were producing an animation for a client, you would be expected to produce evidence to show how you intended to meet the needs of the client. The plans you produced would form an integral part of this evidence.

Storyboarding is an excellent tool which allows you to combine both a visual plan, showing what is going on in the animation, as well as giving evidence of when things are going to happen. A well-produced storyboard should give any client a clear indication of the structure and content of the completed animation.

An example storyboard is available in the Unit 20 Resources zip file which can be downloaded from the OCR Nationals in ICT (Units 2 & 20) Student Resources page on the Payne-Gallway website: www.payne-gallway.co.uk.

How this assessment objective will be assessed...

- As with other assessment objectives, you will need to give a detailed description of your plans if you are to be given a higher grade.
- The quality of your storyboard will also be assessed and, for higher grades, will need to include most if not all of the elements which eventually feature in your completed animation.
- Lastly, you will need to provide a well-structured design which covers most aspects of your plans.

TIP

Your planning does not need to cover every frame. If you concentrate on the main frames, where something is happening, then this will be enough. As we shall see in the next chapter, these are going to be the parts of the animation where you use keyframes.

Skills to use...

The key skills are imagination and understanding of what the software can do. You will be working through an example as you read this and the next chapter and so will have a clear understanding of what is possible with the software. When you come to plan your own animation, use your imagination but at the same time be realistic about what you will achieve.

How to achieve...

Pass requirements

P1 You will describe the aim of the animation.

P2 You will produce a simple storyboard covering the main elements of the animation.

P3 The design itself may lack structure.

Merit requirements

M1 You will describe the aim and audience of the animation.

M2 You will produce a storyboard covering the main elements of the animation.

M3 The design has a clear structure.

Distinction requirements

D1 You will produce a thorough description of the aim and audience of the animation.

D2 You will produce a storyboard covering all elements of the animation.

D3 The design is well structured.

Designing an animation

Before you create your animation, you will need to do some planning. The following sections focus on different tasks and techniques you need to follow as part of this process.

Describing the aim of an animation

We discussed identifying the aim of an animation in the previous chapter and you will have used the points made to identify the aims of the animations which you reviewed. Now that you have reviewed work done by other people, you need to use this understanding to decide on the aim of the animation you will produce.

Your description of the aims of the animation must make it clear what the animation is intended to do. A clear, simple statement at the start of your planning document should be enough.

Describing the audience for an animation

Target audiences were discussed on page 6. You will also have discussed the target audience for the animations you reviewed in the previous chapter.

Your planning document needs to include a clear statement which explains who the target audience is for your animation. You may want to include some discussion of how you intend to appeal to that target audience. This may be a simple table showing what sort of images, or what sort of language, you will use. If you are aiming at one main target audience and also a secondary audience, you should make it clear that there are two target audiences and how you intend to target each.

Choosing the method of animation: tweening or frame-by-frame

You are free to use either tweening or frame-by-frame for your method of animation. This book focuses on the use of Macromedia Flash MX to produce a tweened animation. However, if you are working with frame-by-frame software, there will still be much of interest to you.

You will need to have a clear statement about which method of animation you are going to use to create your animation.

Presenting this information

You will probably have noticed that that each of the items above (the aim, the audience and the method of animation) needs a clear statement as evidence that you have completed this stage of the task. When your work is assessed, the examiner will be looking for each of the above items to be addressed. The simplest method of doing this would be to have a table at the start of your report which answers each one.

Design issue	Comment
Aim of the animation	To add interest to a website by adding movement, sound and animation.
Target audience	People aged between 18 and 25 who may be interested on going on a mountain biking holiday.
Method of animation	Tweening using Flash MX.

You may also wish to show the **frame rate** of your animation. We will discuss this further in Chapter 10 (Assessment Objective 3), but this is basically how many frames you will show per second. Normally, this will be 12 frames per second.

Creating a storyboard

This is where you get creative. A storyboard tells the story of an animation as it progresses. Normally, this would show the main events in the animation. If, for example, you had a person walking down the road, you would not need to create a storyboard for every step but would complete one for each key event. This key event may be a change of camera angle or maybe when something happens to the person, for example, they find a lost wallet or fall down a hole.

The simplest way to produce a storyboard is to have a template which you print off and complete in pencil. Do not worry if your art skills are poor; a storyboard is not a published document and may be drawn with stick people if necessary – a block with two half circles can represent a car, while a square and a triangle make an excellent house!

Your storyboard will need to include:
- content
- text, images, sound and video
- timings
- transitions
- effects.

Content

It should be clear from your storyboard what is included in each frame or group of frames. This may be clear from the quality of your art. If not, notes can be added to your work to make it clearer.

Text, images, sound and video

If you are planning to use any of these elements in your finished animation, they must appear in your storyboard. Remember that your storyboard should include sufficient detail for any client for whom you are working, so that they can imagine what the final animation will look like when finished. A simple rule is that if it is going to go in the animation, it must be on the storyboard. There should be very little difference between the design and content on the storyboard and the design and content of the completed animation.

As we said above, you do not have to use excellent drawing skills when creating a storyboard. A solid block showing the location of a video, with a description of the content of the video, or a draft of a piece of text with a note stating the font type and size is clear evidence of planning.

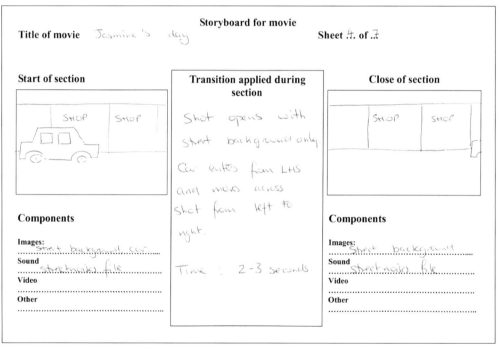

Figure 9.1: *A page from a storyboard showing the use of notes.*

Timings

As you know, animation is the movement of objects from one place to another over a period of time. Your storyboard will show the key events in your animation and so will make it clear how objects will move around your animation. However, you must also show that you have included timing in your planning. If you have made it clear what your frame rate will be, you could show the frame at which each key event will occur (this is the method shown in the example above). Alternatively, you could simply show time in seconds.

Whichever method you choose, your timings should be clearly shown on each page of the storyboard.

Transitions

Transitions are the methods used to change from one scene of an animation to another. You will probably have used these if you have looked at **presentation software** in other areas of ICT. These are basically a set of effects, such as **box in**, or **box out**, which swap the current scene on the screen for the next scene.

Some versions of Flash include **behaviours** which control how elements behave. These may be used to set transitions. However, you could create your own transitions. A transition such as **cover down**, for example, can be created by moving a black object which covers the whole of the screen as the animation moves from one scene to another.

Effects

'**Effects**' refers to the animations you plan to apply to objects on the screen. You might be planning to zoom your text in from the centre, in which case you would add a note to the text explaining that this was your plan. Alternatively, you might be planning to use a motion path to move an image from the left of your screen to the right. Again, a note, with some indication of the motion path on the page, would make it clear that you have included effects in your planning.

How does this apply to Sam's website?

If you have not already done so, download the file **storyboardforSam'sanimation** from the Payne-Gallway website. The storyboard is also available in the appendix (see page 147).

Look through each page and note how the tricks described above have been used to create a clear and usable plan for the animation.

Activity 1: Creating a storyboard for your animation...

In this activity you will:

● create a storyboard for your website.

▶ If you have not done so already, download the Storyboard template and Storyboard Overview template from the Payne-Gallway website.

▶ Print off as many copies as you think you will need for your storyboard and overview.

▶ Use the templates to create your storyboard – remember to include all the elements that will appear in your animation as discussed throughout this chapter.

▶ Check through your finished storyboard and make sure that your planning of each element is clear to see through your use of annotations and artwork.

CHAPTER 10

→ Assessment Objective 3

Create an Animation

Overview:

In this chapter you will be shown how to create an animation. You will use your skills to combine together the elements we discussed in Chapter 9 to create an animation of 15 seconds length, if you are aiming for a **Pass** grade, or 30 seconds, if you are aiming for **Merit** or **Distinction**. Your animation will be fit for purpose and, whichever level you are working at, must be saved in a format suitable for use on the Internet.

In order to complete the activities in this chapter you will need access to a number of additional files. These files are contained in the Unit 20 Resources zip file which can be downloaded from the OCR Nationals in ICT (Units 2 & 20) Student Resources page on the Payne-Gallway website: www.payne-gallway.co.uk.

How this assessment objective will be assessed...

- The first issue will be the length of your animation. If you are aiming for anything other than a **Pass**, your animation must be at least 30 seconds long.
- The second issue will be the range of skills you use to produce your completed animation.
- If you are able to show that you can make good use of:
  - o basic graphic techniques
  - o tweening or frame-by-frame animation
  - o frame rates
  - o looping

  then you will be working at **Distinction** level.
- You will be assessed on how well your elements work.
- To achieve a **Distinction** grade, your presentation must be optimised.

Skills to use...

In Assessment Objective 3 you produce your Flash animation. Your planning will give you an idea of what the final product should look like but now is where you show your skills in drawing and animating. Your work will need to be accurate and of a high standard. When you have completed your animation, your work will need to download quickly and easily; as you create the animation, bear in mind that you need to keep the overall file size to a minimum.

How to achieve...

Pass requirements

P1 You must create an animation which lasts for at least 15 seconds.

P2 You must make use of basic graphic techniques and tweening or frame-by-frame animation when creating the animation. Some of the elements might not work as intended.

P3 The animation will be exported in a suitable file format for use on the web.

Merit requirements

M1 You must create an animation which lasts for at least 30 seconds.

M2 The animation must be appropriate.

M3 The animation will make good use of:
  o basic graphic techniques
  o tweening or frame-by-frame animation
  o frame rates
  o looping.

M4 Most of the completed animation will work as intended, but there may be some elements which do not work as intended.

M5 The animation will be exported in a suitable file format for use on the web.

Distinction requirements

D1 You must create an animation which lasts for at least 30 seconds.

D2 The animation must be appropriate and meet the identified aims.

D3 The animation will make good use of:
  o basic graphic techniques
  o tweening or frame-by-frame animation
  o frame rates
  o looping.

D4 All of the elements will work as intended.

D5 The animation will be optimised and exported in a suitable file format for use on the web.

An introduction to Flash

In this chapter, we will concentrate on using **Macromedia Flash 8** to produce tweened animations.

Flash is a great piece of software which is mostly used to create animations. However, it can be used to create vector graphics as well as interactive elements, such as buttons, for websites.

Flash works with a main stage area into which you place resources. These resources may have been imported into the software, such as images or videos, or may be created, using the range of drawing tools which are available within the software. Flash uses **layers** to separate these resources. Layers operate very much like OHP sheets, with elements being grouped onto sheets and then laid on top of other sheets. When you first create a Flash document, there will be one layer only. However, as you add resources, you will need to add extra layers so that different elements may be animated separately.

If you imagine that someone was using OHP sheets and wanted to create the illusion of movement, they may move the OHP sheet from one side to another. Flash allows you to do exactly the same. If you wanted to create an animation of a car moving from left to right in front of a row of houses, you would create the background layer, which would have the houses on it, and then create a layer which held the car. You would then apply the animation to this layer only, so that the car moved relative to the background. This would create the illusion of movement.

Flash uses a **timeline** to show different stages of the animation. This timeline plays from left to right and is shown by a **playhead** – the red line shown on the screenshot below – which moves across the page. To get a better feel for what is happening in your animation, you can click on the playhead and drag it along the timeline. As you move the playhead, so elements and effects appear on the screen as the playhead reaches them.

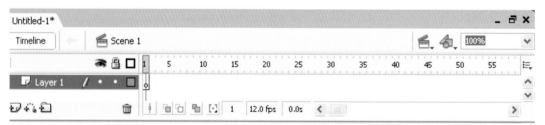

Figure 10.1: *The Flash timeline and layer 1.*

Key terms

Timeline

The line which represents time passing.

Playhead

Moves from left to right along the timeline as time passes.

Renaming layers

New layers are named in the order in which they are created. However, you can rename layers so that they have more meaningful names. If you do use meaningful names for each layer, this will make your work better organised. This will not only make it easier for you to work with layers but will mean that anybody reviewing your work will get a better impression.

There are a number of ways to rename a layer. By far the most simple is to double click on the name and enter a new name.

The project

As you work through this chapter, you will be working on a project to create an animation to be included in Sam's website. This will allow you to practise the skills you need to create an animation of your own. You saw the plan for this animation in the previous chapter on page 113. The screenshot below shows a frame towards the end of this animation.

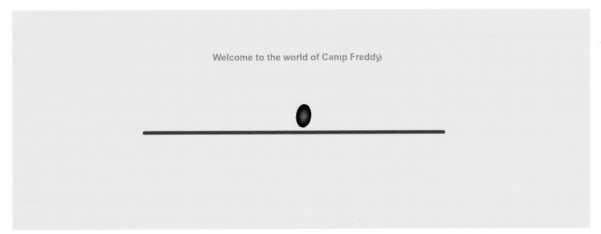

Figure 10.2: *The completed animation.*

You will create this animation as you work through this chapter. So that the work you produce is the correct size, you should use the **rulers** which Flash provides. The default setting is for rulers to show pixels. When you first open Flash, rulers are not switched on, so you should switch these on by selecting **view...rulers** when you have opened a new Flash document.

Getting started

No doubt you want to get on with using the software. Before you do though, remember that theory is important too, so you will need to pay attention to some of the 'whys' as well as the 'hows'!

Open the software by:

- *either* clicking on the icon 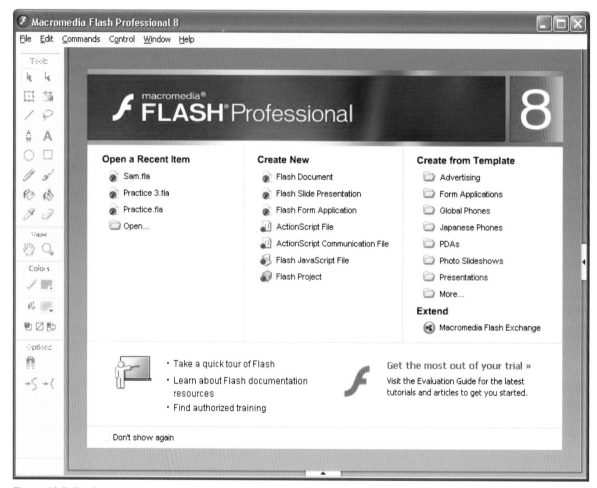, if it is on your desktop
- *or* opening it from the programs list on your computer. If you are working on your own computer, this will be in the folder called Macromedia. However, if you are working on a machine in your centre, Flash may be grouped in with other animation or web authoring software.
- Flash opens to the start page.

Figure 10.3: *The Flash start page.*

Creating a new document

When the start page opens, you will see a lot of options and features set up in different **panels**. Each of these panels is linked to a specific feature of Flash. Do not worry – you will soon become very used to working with them.

Click on **Create new Flash document** icon on the start page.

The start page will close and a new page will come up. This is probably even more confusing than the previous one but, again, you will soon get used to it. There are four main elements on this new page. These are:

* **the stage** – this is the big white area in the centre of the screen. The grey area around the stage is the **work area**. These two areas are where you place all of the resources which will make up your animation
* **the timeline** – this is a visual representation of the timing of your animation. As the animation plays, so the red marker moves to the right
* **the toolbar** – this appears on the left of the screen and is shown in Figure 10.4
* **the panels** – these cover up parts of your screen and can be turned off, maximised or minimised as you wish. If you minimise a panel, this lets you see more of the stage. Panels can be maximised or minimised by clicking anywhere in the light blue bar. The properties panel for a new document is shown below.

Figure 10.4: *The Flash toolbar.*

Figure 10.5: *The properties panel.*

Activity 1: Create a practice Flash document…

In this activity you will:

* make some changes to your first Flash document.

The Flash document you have created above will, by default, have one layer called **Layer 1**. We will use this layer to hold the background. The background should be light green.

▶ Open the properties panel for your new document and click on the Background window (in the middle of the panel). This will open the Flash colour palette. As you move your mouse over the palette, so the window at the top changes to show a code for each colour you pass. Choose #00FF00.

▶ Rename this layer **background**.

▶ Your document needs to be 550 pixels wide and 250 pixels high.

▶ Save this file as **practice**.

A note about using and choosing colours in Flash

Before we go any further, we need to discuss how you use colours when working with Flash. Unlike Microsoft products, when you work with colours, Flash gives you a palette of 420 colours from which to choose. When choosing colours, your cursor becomes a dropper. As your dropper moves over a colour, you are also given a six-digit colour code in the top window. This is called the **hexadecimal** value for the colour. We will use these values when we are talking about colours. To find a specific colour, you can either move the cursor over the colour palette or type the hexadecimal value, beginning with the #, into the window at the top of the palette.

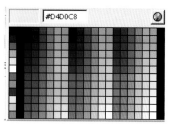

Figure 10.6: Choose a colour, any colour.

However, when you come to produce your own animation, you may be given a **Red, Green, Blue** value for any colours you are expected to use. You can set these values in a second colour palette by clicking on the colour wheel icon at the top right of the hexadecimal palette.

When working with objects, as well as choosing colours, you can choose preset colour effects from the menu at the bottom of the palette. These will not only apply colour to your shape, but will also use shading to create a shape which appears three dimensional.

> ⏺**TIP**
>
> You do not have to use one of the colours included in the palette but can move your cursor (the dropper) to clone any colour on the screen.

Animation editing techniques

We will now move on to discuss the different animation techniques which you can use when working with Flash MX.

Basic techniques 1: drawing and editing shapes

We have already said that Flash can be used to create vector graphics. In the activity below, you are going to learn how to create basic vector graphic shapes. We will move on to working on Sam's animation once you have learnt how to create some basic shapes.

Activity 2: Creating shapes...

In this activity you will:

● learn how to create a simple oval with a yellow fill colour and a blue edge.

▶ Create a new Flash document.

▶ Click on the **oval/circle** tool ⬭ .

▶ Colours are part of the properties of the shape. Open the **properties panel**.

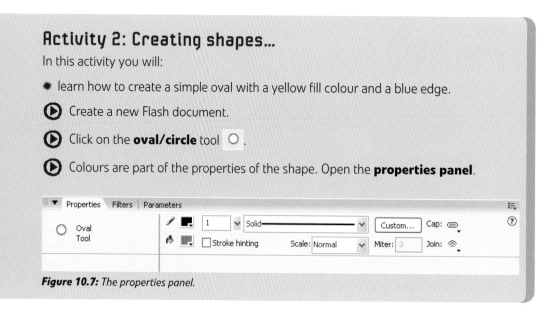

Figure 10.7: The properties panel.

▶ The colour by the pen icon is the stroke or pen colour, while the colour by the tin of paint icon (this looks like the flood fill icon you may have seen in other software titles) is the fill colour. Click on the **pen icon** and choose dark blue colour (#000066). Click on the **flood fill** icon and choose yellow colour (#FFFF00).

▶ Hold down the **left mouse button** and draw your oval.

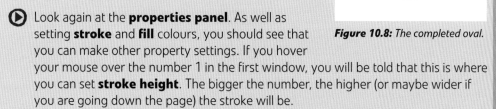

▶ You can also create a rectangle using the **rectangle** tool. If you want to draw a square, hold down the **shift** key as you draw.

▶ Look again at the **properties panel**. As well as setting **stroke** and **fill** colours, you should see that you can make other property settings. If you hover

Figure 10.8: The completed oval.

your mouse over the number 1 in the first window, you will be told that this is where you can set **stroke height**. The bigger the number, the higher (or maybe wider if you are going down the page) the stroke will be.

▶ You should also see a window with the word **Solid** and a solid line. If you hover over this window, you will be told that this is where you can set the **Stroke style**. If you select the downhill arrow to the right of this window, you will see that there are seven options from which you can choose.

▶ The final option is to look into the **custom options**. You should use this option if you want to use other property settings.

Key terms

Stroke color

This refers to the colour of the pen which draws the outline of any shape.

Fill color

This refers to the colour which is used to fill a shape.

⊘**TIP**

Spend a few moments playing with the options included in the custom menu.

The select tools

Now that you have used Flash to draw an oval, you can also edit any shape you have created. To do so, you will need to use the select tools.

Flash has two select tools:
- the **select arrow** ▸ (this is used to select part of a shape)
- the **selection box**.

The next two activities will show you how to use each of these tools.

Activity 3: Using the select arrow...

In this activity you will:

● use the select arrow to change the outline and fill colours of your oval.

▶ Choose the select arrow from the toolbar.

▶ Click on the dark blue border of the oval. You should see a dotted line around the shape. If the whole of the shape is dotted, click **Esc** to cancel and try again.

▶ Open the **properties** panel if it is not already open. You will notice that the **fill color** shows a white box with a red line through it. This shows that this option is not available, which makes sense as you are working on the border colour and not the fill colour. Click on the **stroke color** box and choose colour #FF0000. The oval will now have a red border.

Extension

▶ You can change the fill colour by clicking on the inside of the oval. In this case, the **stroke color** will not be available.

▶ You may also want to change more than one element of a shape at a time. For example, you may want to change both the **stroke color** and **fill color** properties. To select both the inside and the border, hold down the **shift key**.

Activity 4: Using the selection box...

In this activity you will:

● use a selection box to select part of the oval you have created and to edit it.

You have decided that rather than have an oval, you would rather have a half oval.

▶ Choose the select arrow.

▶ Click to the left of the oval and hold down the left mouse button.

▶ Drag to the right until the left half of the oval has been selected.

▶ Hit the **delete** button. The left-hand side of the oval will now have disappeared.

Extension

You can work with the area you have selected in exactly the same way as you did above. You could, for example, change the fill colour so that the selected area has a different fill colour to the area which has not been selected.

How does this apply to Sam's website?

You will now start a new Flash document. You will work with this document to create the animation for Sam's website.

Activity 5: Creating a Flash document for Sam's website...

In this activity you will:

● create a Flash document which will be used for the animation for Sam's website.

▶ Create a new Flash document with a yellow (#FFFF00) background, which is 550 pixels wide and 300 pixels high. Save your document as **Sam** and rename **Layer 1** as **background**. You will need the ruler on (**View...rulers**) and **scale** (at the top right of the page) set to **100%**.

▶ You will now create the ball which rolls along the line on the animation. You will use the pre-set red fill colour.

▶ Create a new layer by using **one** of the following methods below. You can *either*:

● click on the **Insert Layer** button at the bottom of the timeline *or*
● select **Insert...Timeline...Layer** *or*
● right click on a layer in the timeline and choose **Insert Layer** from the drop-down menu which appears.

▶ Name this layer **ball**.

▶ Choose the **oval tool** and the **pre-set red fill** from the flood fill menu. Make sure that **stroke height** is 1 and choose #000000 for the **stroke colour**.

▶ Click on the left-hand side of the page, at about point 125 on the **y-axis** and 50 on the **x-axis**. Hold the left mouse button down, and draw a circle by moving the cursor to point 150 on the **y-axis**, 75 on the **x-axis**.

Figure 10.9: The right-click drop-down menu.

▶ You will now have a ball on your screen. You may notice that it does not look quite like the ball which is shown on the screenshot at the start of this chapter. This is because the ball in the final animation has been skewed using the **free transform** tool. We will look at how the free transform tool may be used to do this later in this chapter.

Working with levels

The ball you have just created is what is called a **stage level object**. Objects at this level are a collection of strokes and fills. This means that you can click on a part of the shape and drag it away or change the colour. The bits you have not clicked on will not move or change. This makes it easy to edit parts of a shape but can also lead to mistakes!

Once your shape is complete, you will normally want it to be treated as a single shape, rather than a group of parts. This is done by moving your shape to the **overlay level**. Any shapes which exist on the overlay level are treated as complete shapes and cannot be broken up into their constituent parts.

Changing a stage level object into an overlay level object

There are two ways to change a stage level object into an overlay level object. You can:

- *either* **group** the object – this is simply a case of selecting the object and choosing **group** from the **modify menu**

Figure 10.10: *The modify menu.*

- *or* change the object into a **symbol**. This is done by choosing **convert to symbol** from the **modify menu**. The **convert to symbol** dialogue box will appear.

Figure 10.11: *The convert to symbol dialogue box.*

This dialogue box offers you three types of symbol. Each type has a range of different behaviours. You should choose the type which best suits what you want to do with the symbol. If you are creating an image which does nothing but look pretty, choose **Graphic**. If your symbol is going to be a button, then choose **Button**. The **Movie clip** option is for symbols which will have some animation and maybe some sound.

Grouped objects versus symbols

You are probably wondering what the difference is between grouped objects and symbols. Both types of element are **overlay** objects and so cannot be broken up. However, **symbols** are automatically added to the **library**. Elements in the library are inserted into a piece of animation as an **instance**, which basically means that the software knows where the symbol is stored; whenever the symbol is used, the software checks in the library to see what it looks like and copies it onto the page. This means that your animation will have a far smaller file size, as the symbol is saved once, however many times it is used.

This has a second benefit. Because the software goes to look at the symbol in the library whenever it is used, if you change the appearance of a symbol, this change will come into effect wherever the symbol is used.

Activity 6: Grouping the oval...

In this activity you will:

● learn how to group an object.

▶ Use the selection tool to draw a **selection box** around the red ball you have just created.

▶ Select **modify...group**.

▶ The ball should now have a blue box around it. (If you select any **overlay object**, it automatically has a blue box around it. So, if your ball now has a blue box, it is an overlay object and you must have been successful.)

▶ Now that you have grouped your ball, you can click on it and move it to anywhere on the stage as one object.

⊙TIP

Do not confuse layers and levels. Layers are like the OHP sheets we discussed above and are where elements sit in the animation. Levels refer to the type of element.

Basic techniques 2: lines

When you are working in Flash, lines are treated as strokes. This makes sense if you think about it because, so far, you have used lines to create shapes and then used a **fill colour** to give the shape an internal colour. Lines do not have internal colour, so only a stroke is needed.

Lines are an object on the page, just like ovals and rectangles. You will not be surprised to know that lines have properties, just like any other object on the page. This means that you can make the same changes to the properties of a line as you can to the properties of a rectangle or oval.

How does this apply to Sam's website?

You are now going to create the line along which the ball rolls. In this animation, the ball appears to move, while the line remains in one place. This means that the line and the ball must be on separate layers.

Activity 7: Creating a line...

In this activity you will:

● create a line for the ball to roll along.

▶ Insert a new layer and call this **line**.

▶ Choose the **line** tool and, using the settings in the properties panel, create a horizontal line which has the following properties:

- ● stroke colour #0000FF
- ● stroke height 5
- ● stroke style solid
- ● width 450.

▶ Group the line so that it moves to the **overlay layer**.

▶ Move the line so that the left-hand end is at point 150 on the **y-axis** and 50 on the **x-axis**. Select the ball and move it so that it sits just on the line on the left-hand side. As you move the ball near to the line, the software provides you with helpful layout guides which you can use to properly position your ball.

Figure 10.12: *The circle and line.*

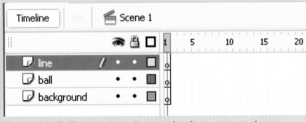

Figure 10.13: *The timeline, showing the three separate layers.*

> ⊘TIP
>
> You can add elements to layers by selecting that layer on the timeline. This means that if you want to come back and add an element to a layer, it is simply a case of clicking on the layer and importing the element.

Using the free transform tool

One very important edit which you can make to a shape is to change the size. As we have discussed, the elements you create using either the oval, rectangle and line tools are all vector graphic images. If you know anything about **vector graphics**, you should remember that they are very easy to resize without any distortion. This is especially true when you make vector graphics larger.

Flash includes a really useful tool, which is the **free transform tool** . This tool allows you to resize objects, as well as distort their shape.

When you select an object with the **free transform tool**, the object will surrounded by a box which has eight small boxes, one at each corner and one on each side. These are called **handles**. Handles can be used to drag and resize the shape. However, the free transform tool also offers a further facility, which is the **skew tool**. With this tool, you are able to twist and distort the selected shape. To access this tool, click on the outside of the shape between the handles and drag.

How does this apply to Sam's website?

The ball you created needs to be distorted slightly. We will use the **free transform tool** to **skew** this graphic. The 'before' and 'after' balls are shown below.

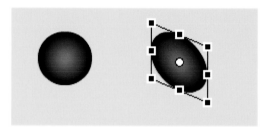

Figure 10.14: *The ball before and after being skewed.*

Activity 8: Using the free transform tool to skew an image...

In this activity you will:

● skew the ball you created.

▶ Before you start, you will need to zoom in closer so that you can work with the ball. Change the zoom (at the top right of the screen) to 200%.

▶ The red ball is on the **ball** layer. Left click with the mouse to select this layer.

▶ Select the red ball you created by clicking on it with the mouse.

▶ Select the **free transform tool**. A black box with handles will now appear around the object.

▶ Click on the bottom right vertical part of this black outline box (the segment between east and south east if you were using a compass).

> ⊘TIP
>
> The Free Transform tool cannot be applied to text, symbols, bitmap images, video objects, sounds or gradients.

▶ Hold the left mouse button down and drag down until the middle handle is above where the bottom right handle was. You should see the ball skew down towards the bottom of your screen.

▶ When you have completed the skew, click away from the skewed red ball to deselect the object. You may need to reposition the ball above the line.

▶ Do not forget to change the zoom back to 100% when you have completed this task.

Basic techniques 3: using text

The first thing to point out is that, unlike rectangles, ovals and lines, text is automatically an **overlay level object**. This means that you do not have to worry about any text you create being split up. However, if you do want text to be **stage level**, you can right click it when you are working with the select tool and choose **break apart** from the menu which appears.

Activity 9: Adding text to an animation...

In this activity you will:

● add the text at the top of your animation.

▶ You will need the ruler switched on for this task. Switch this facility on now if it is not already shown on your screen.

▶ Create a new layer and name this **text**.

▶ Select the **text tool** and open the properties panel.

▶ The design shows that the text needs to be:

- Arial font
- font size 10
- fill colour #0099CC
- bold.

Once completed, your properties panel should look like this:

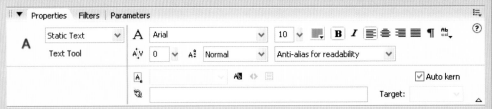

Figure 10.15: The tool properties panel.

▶ Now click above the line and ball and type:

Welcome to the world of Camp Freddy!

▶ Your text needs to be placed in the centre of the page with the baseline of the text 50 pixels down from the top. Use the **selection** tool to drag the text to the correct position on the page.

Figure 10.16: Your animation with text added.

Importing objects

Up to now, you have created elements for use in the animation. The design for Sam's animation includes some images of the band. These need to be **imported** into the **library**.

You should already have downloaded the images for this stage of creating the animation. These images are called:

- **1small.jpg**
- **2small.jpg**
- **3small.jpg**

Each of these files has been given the prefix 'small' because they have been resized ready for use on the animation. As we discussed in the section on optimising images for use on websites on page 52, reducing the size of an image in a graphics package will reduce the file size and so will reduce the amount of time required to download the animation and the website on which it is housed.

You will now **import** these images into your **library**. Once in the library, you will be free to use these objects on your animation.

Activity 10: Importing objects...

In this activity you will:

- import objects into your library.

▶ Choose **import** from the **file** drop-down menu.

▶ Choose **import to library** from the import menu.

▶ Navigate to the folder where your images are stored.

▶ Select the images you wish to import. A quick way of selecting all images is to select the first image, hold down the shift key and then, using the down arrow on the keyboard, move down through the list of images.

▶ Click **open**. Your images will now be in your library. If your library panel is not open, it can be opened by selecting **Library** from the **Window** drop-down panel.

Figure 10.17: *The library with all three image elements added.*

Importing video

The animation you are creating for Sam does not include video. However, video is one element of multimedia presentations which you could choose to use with your final animation. The method used to import video is very much like the method used to import other elements. However, when you try to import a video, Flash picks up on this and sends out the **Video Import** Wizard to help you. This wizard offers the opportunity to:

- **embed** your video in the Flash file or **link to the source**
- edit the video before it is imported
- apply compression to your video based on bandwidth and quality settings.

Linking brings problems and so it is better to embed any video with the rest of your Flash animation. Embedding videos also allows you to set compression rates for the video.

⊙TIP

You can test any video files you have placed in your animation by dragging the playhead along the timeline. However, this will provide visuals only. If you want to hear the sound, you will have to use the Test Movie facility.

Video file types

Flash cannot work with all video file types although the main types are compatible. If you want further information about the precise video formats with which Flash is compatible, you should check the extensive list included in the Flash help files.

Cutting, copying and pasting

Flash allows you to cut, copy and paste individual objects, as well as whole frames or groups of frames.

The tool is very much like every other cut, copy and paste facility you have used, except that you are given the option to paste the copied object:

- in the centre of the page
- in the same location as the original
- as a paste special, where you can choose the format of the pasted object.

These tools are all available from the **Edit** drop-down menu. Any object copied using these tools can only be pasted into frames which already exist.

Individual or groups of frames may be copied by selecting with the mouse and then using the right click drop-down menu.

Tweening

Now we come to the really flash bit of Flash! This is where you learn to animate the objects on your stage. Flash has two types of animation: **motion tweening** and **shape tweening**. When Flash creates a 'tween', it creates the movement between two frames on the animation. This reduces the amount of work the author has to do and therefore makes tweened animation a far easier form of animation than **frame-by-frame** animation. Shape tweening is described on page 134 whilst motion tweening is explored below.

Motion tweening

Motion tweening happens between two physical places on the stage over time. When you create a motion tween, you need to set both the beginning and end position for the object, as well as the beginning and end time over which the movement will take place. This is probably best explained with the use of an example.

Imagine an animation moving a picture of a car from the left of the screen to the right. The start position would be on the left of the screen and the end on the right. However, this is only half of the information. The movement from left to right will start at frame 30 and take 60 frames to complete. This means that the movement will be complete by frame 90.

We would therefore say that the car moves from left to right between frames 30 and 90.

Tweening can only be applied to grouped objects or symbols. When planning animation, it is also better to have each tweened object occupying a layer of its own. To avoid confusion, it is a good idea to give tween effects a name so that different effects may be found on your timeline. This is done by entering a name in the **frame label** window on the **properties panel**. Each effect must have a unique name.

How to set the beginning and end of an animation

The beginning and end of a section on the timeline are shown by **keyframes**. Keyframes are basically important frames where something happens. When creating animations, keyframes show when an animation starts to occur and the end. When you first create a Flash animation, you will find only one keyframe, which will be at frame 1. However, as you work through your animation, so you will add any number of keyframes which show when different events in your animation occur.

If you think back to the animation of the car, you should understand that there will be a keyframe at frame 30, which will be the beginning of the animation, and another at frame 90, which will be the end of the animation.

The screenshot below shows a keyframe at frame 30 and another at frame 60.

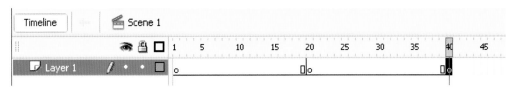

Figure 10.18: *Two keyframes on a timeline.*

You can add a keyframe by right clicking on the timeline where you want the event to occur. This would be a specific frame. If you have more than one layer, you will need to select the layer with which you are working. Choose **Insert keyframe** from the context menu which appears.

Figure 10.19: *The right click context menu.*

Key terms

Keyframes

These are important frames which show the beginning and end of sections of the timeline.

How does this apply to Sam's website?

We will now apply the **motion tween** to the ball so that it moves from left to right along the line and then back to the beginning.

At the moment, both the line and the ball are in frame 1 only. You are about to apply animation to the ball which will, eventually, make it animate all the way up to frame 180. If you are not careful, the line will only be on the screen for one frame only, which is not what you need at all.

Activity 11: Set the ball rolling...

In this activity you will:

● apply motion tween to the ball to make it move along the line.

▶ Before you apply any animation to the ball, select the **line layer** and right click on **frame 180**. Insert a **keyframe** at this point.

Flash will now have extended the grey area, which shows how long the line will be on the screen, all the way out to frame 180.

We need to tell the software that the ball is going to move from the left-hand side of the blue line in the animation to the right-hand side of the blue line in the animation.

▶ Select the ball layer. Using the **select tool**, click on the ball. (If you cannot see it, you are probably in frame 180 – don't forget that the ball exists in frame 1 only.)

▶ Right click **frame 30** and select **Insert keyframe**.

▶ Click on the ball to select it and drag it to the far right-hand side of the blue line. Use the helpful guide line to move the ball horizontally across the page and not down.

▶ Click on any frame between 1 and 29 (make sure you click on the layer which holds the ball).

You will now change the settings on the **properties panel** to make the ball roll from left to right.

Figure 10.20: *The properties panel.*

▶ From the **properties panel**, select **motion** from the tween drop-down menu. Flash will now draw an arrow headed line from frame 1 to frame 29. If you do not get an arrow, but a dotted line, this shows that a motion tween has been applied but that there is an error. This error may be that you have tried to tween ungrouped shapes or that there is some sort of disruption in the animation, such as extra keyframes. If you hit a problem, you can try to fix it by removing elements which are interfering. Alternatively (and probably a better option when you first start working with Flash) you could delete the whole layer and start the layer again.

Figure 10.21: *A successfully applied motion tween.*

Now you are going make the ball roll. This looks great but is very simple. The trick here is to not let anyone know how easy it is!

▶ From the **properties panel**, select **CW** (clockwise) from the **rotate** drop-down menu and enter **4** for the amount of times. This will make the ball roll in a clockwise manner four times as it rolls along. You should now be starting to appreciate what a step forward in animation tweening really is! Name this effect **roll forward**. This name will now appear on the timeline.

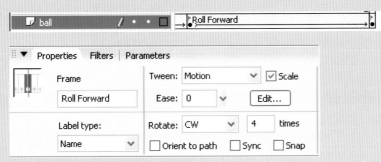

Figure 10.22: *The added label.*

Finally, you need to make the ball move from the right back to the left.

▶ Click on **frame 60** and insert a new keyframe. (Remember that we are working with the **ball** layer.) Flash will automatically create a grey area from frame 30 to frame 59.

▶ With the **select tool** chosen, click on the ball and drag the ball back to the original starting position on the far left-hand side of the blue line. Again, make sure that the ball moves horizontally across the page.

▶ Click anywhere between frames 30 and 59 and create a motion path which rotates the ball four times in a **CCW** (counter clockwise) direction. Name this effect **roll back**.

▶ You have now created an animation which covers 60 frames. You should now repeat the steps twice more so that this animation covers 180 frames. Remember to use unique names for each effect – maybe you could use **'roll forward 1'** and then **'roll forward 2'**. These names are both meaningful and unique.

TIP

You can test your animation by selecting control…test movie. To get back to your work area, close the Flash player window.

Easing

Movement tweening is a great effect. You have just been shown quite a simple motion tween but there are other effects you could try. **Easing** is a way to make your animation speed up or slow down. This is set to zero by default but you should experiment with changing this setting to a negative or a positive figure. You should also experiment with changing colours of objects as the motion tween occurs.

Shape tweening

Shape tweening follows exactly the same theory as **motion tweening** and is just as easy. The basic idea of shape tweening is that you have a clear shape at one point in your timeline, but by the time that your playhead reaches a later time, the shape has changed to something different. The choice of how different is up to you. Your shape could be completely different or could just be the same shape made bigger or with some other small effect applied.

Just like with motion tweening, you set the beginning shape up at the first frame and the final shape in the last frame.

How does this apply to Sam's website?

The text you inserted needs to appear and zoom in. This is a classic piece of shape tweening. This is achieved by setting up your original text at one point on the timeline and then setting up what the text will look like at another point. So that Flash can do the tweening, you will need to use the **ungroup** command to break the text up.

Activity 12: Using shape tweening...

In this activity you will:

- apply shape tweening to text.

▶ At the moment, your text appears in **frame 1**. Our plan shows that it does not need to appear until **frame 30**. Select the layer which holds the text. Right click on **frame 30** and insert a keyframe. Flash will automatically insert a greyed area from **frame 1** to **frame 30**.

▶ Click on **frame 1** and, holding the left mouse button down, drag to the right to select all frames forward to **frame 29**. Right click and select **clear frames** from the drop-down menu which appears. The text **Welcome to the world of Camp Freddy** will now have been removed from frames 1 to 29 and will only appear in **frame 30**.

▶ Stay on the text layer and insert a keyframe at **frame 90**. If you run the playhead over the animation, the text will now be on the screen from frames 30 to 90.

▶ So that the new text can go on the page, left click to select **frame 90**. Use the **select tool** to highlight and then delete the text at this frame.

▶ Use the **text tool** to add the text **Welcome to the world of Camp Freddy**. This should be:

- in **Arial** font
- **font size 26**
- centred on the page
- with the bottom of the text still on **50** on the **y-axis**
- in bold.

(▶) Use the select tool to move this new piece of text if it is in the wrong place.

(▶) Select **Modify…break apart** to break the text up. Because of the way Flash works with text, Flash will have broken the text up into letters. This is so that individual letters could have an effect applied. You will want to go further than this, so repeat the **Modify…break apart** step again.

> ⊘ **TIP**
>
> The plan says that the fill colour should again be #0099CC, but you could experiment with changing the colour at this stage.

(▶) Select **frame 30** and repeat step 6 to break up the text at this frame.

(▶) Click between frames 30 and 90 and select **Shape** from the tween drop-down menu.

Further ideas

If you now test your movie, you will see that there is a lot going on. This would be enough for most people but we want more!

We have just looked at using a shape tween to make an object grow. This may be a classic use of this tool but it is not the most exciting. You could try using a shape tween to change one piece of text into another, or part of a message could change, maybe by changing a number into a word ('1' could change to 'one', for example). Another trick you could explore is changing a shape into a letter or a collection of shapes into a word.

Motion guides

A motion guide is a motion tween which is given a specific path to follow. You may have come across this idea when working with some **presentation software** packages. To ensure that your object follows the motion guide, you will need to use **snapping**.

Snapping lets you set an object so that it 'snaps' to aspects of your animation. This may be the grid which covers the stage (this is switched off by default) or may be an object. A motion grid is an object which the image needs to follow, so select **view…snapping…snap to objects**. Snapping is a really useful facility which you will need to explore further on your own.

Activity 13: Creating a motion guide…

In this activity you will:

- learn how to create a motion guide
- apply the motion guide to one image on the Camp Freddy animation.

The plan for the animation includes three small images. One of these images will fly in, while the other two will appear. Before you create the fly in effect, you will insert the two images at **keyframe 91**.

(▶) Create a new layer called **second and third image**.

(▶) Drag **2small.jpg** so that it sits about 30 pixels above the line and about 50 pixels in from the far left-hand side of the blue line (remember to leave enough room for the ball to pass underneath). Repeat with **3small.jpg** but place the image on the far right-hand side of the blue line.

You are now going to insert the image which flies into the animation between the two static images.

▶ Create a new layer and call it **first image**. Flash will automatically expand it to cover the whole length of the animation.

▶ Insert a **keyframe** at frame 91.

▶ Select **1small.jpg** from where it has been waiting patiently in your library and drag it to the far top of your work area, well away from the stage. You are going to create an animation which flies in from the top of the stage.

▶ Insert a **keyframe** at frame 120.

▶ You will now insert the motion guide to take **1small.jpg** from where it is waiting, down onto the stage. Select **Insert...timeline...motion guide**. This will set up a motion guide above the **first image** layer. This motion guide will be prefixed by 'Guide' and then the name of the layer to which it applies, which is helpful.

▶ Make sure you have selected the guide layer and then use the **Pencil tool** to draw your motion path. Your path should end up just above the line at about **100** on the **x-axis**. This path will not appear on the finished product – it is only a guide!

▶ It is a good idea to **lock** your guide so that you do not change it by mistake. There is a lot happening on your page and it is probably getting a bit complicated! The **lock** option is found on the timeline, just to the right of the **layer name**.

▶ Select **frame 91** and drag the image to the start of your motion guide. Because you have **lock to object** switched on, the image will fit tightly onto the start of the motion guide.

▶ Select **frame 120**, select your image and lock it to the end of the motion guide.

▶ Click anywhere between frames 91 and 120 on the **first image** layer and select **motion tween**.

Further ideas

There are some other effects you could use. Timeline effects, which are part of the **Insert** menu, allow you to make objects fade in or out by using the **transition tool**. The **transform tool** allows you to rotate or move a selected object.

Experiment with these tools. Maybe you could use the transition tool to make an object gradually disappear.

Frame rates

We have already explained that each **frame** on the timeline represents a period of time. However, we have not actually said how much time each frame represents. This is because we have not yet discussed **frame rates**. The frame rate is the amount of frames which are shown per second. It is generally accepted that 12 frames per second is the best rate for use on the Internet, but this may differ with certain machines. If you want to be really professional, you should test your completed animation with a variety of different machines so that you may be sure that you are using the best frame rate.

The **frame rate** is set as one of the properties on the **document properties panel**. This is the same panel you used to set the background colour.

The minimum requirement for this qualification is that your animation should last for at least 15 seconds. At a frame rate of 12 frames per second, this is a total of 180 frames. Therefore, the animation you have just created for Sam would be a Pass grade animation.

Key terms

Frame rate

The amount of frames which are played per second.

Looping

The Flash player, which is the software which plays Flash movies, is set to loop any Flash movie it plays. Making a Flash animation *not* loop involves the use of **Action Code**, which goes beyond the space available in this book.

If you wish to add the code to stop a Flash animation looping, a search of the Internet will bring up many websites with explanations of the code to do this.

If you export your animation as an HTML file, you will be given the option of switching looping on or off.

Optimising

If you have read Chapters 1 and 2 of this book, you should know that you need to optimise the elements on a web page so that each page downloads and opens as quickly as possible. The animation you create for this unit is intended for use on the Internet, therefore you should do what you can to optimise these files, just like you would any other elements you include.

Optimising is the process of reducing the amount of data which needs to be downloaded before the **browser** can show the web page. There are two ways of optimising. Firstly, when they are created, web pages use elements which have been downloaded across the Internet. Any image you use on a website is downloaded once, however many times it is used. Use common elements, such as buttons, rather than a different button for every action, or seven different versions of the home button.

Secondly, make sure that each element you use has as small a file size as possible. This is basically a case of reducing the information needed to create the object. When you work with Flash, you can optimise individual elements using the **Modify…Shape** drop-down menu. This tool works by reducing the complexity of a shape, as the more complex a shape, the more information has to be stored for it to be created.

In the case of the ball you created above, the tool cannot do much, as a ball needs to have curves for it to be a ball. However, the more complex a shape, the more opportunity there is to remove extra pieces which are not needed and, therefore, reduce the amount of information needed to create the shape.

Flash includes an easy-to-use analysis tool called the **Bandwidth Profiler**. This is part of the **view** menu when you are previewing your animation. This tool analyses the time it takes to download any animations or movies which are created.

Activity 14: Testing download times...

In this activity you will:

● use the **optimise** tool
● use the **Bandwidth Profiler** to check the effectiveness of the optimise tool.

▶ Create a new Flash file. Right click on the timeline and insert a blank **keyframe**.

▶ Select **frame 1** and, using the **pencil tool**, draw a shape with plenty of curves and lines and circles.

▶ Select **Edit...Copy**. Select **frame 2** and select **Edit...Paste in place** so that both frames hold exactly the same work of art. These frames are identical, so if you apply the **optimise** tool and there is a reduction in the download speed, this must show that the optimise process works.

▶ With **frame 2** selected, select **Modify...Shape...Optimise**. The **Optimize Curves** dialogue box will appear. Now you have to make a decision. If you want to optimise as much as possible, drag the slider to the right. You'll find that you get an optimised picture but you lose curves. If you want to keep the curves, drag the slider to the left. Now you have lots of curves but the picture takes a while to download. You could of course leave the cursor in the middle...

▶ Click **OK** when you are ready to go.

▶ A Flash warning screen will pop up telling you the effect.

Now to test whether the optimisation process has been successful...

▶ Select **Control...Test Movie**. If the **Bandwidth Profiler** is not on, select it from the **View** drop-down menu.

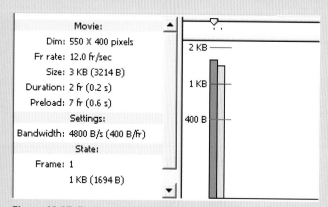

Figure 10.23: *The bandwidth profiler in action.*

If you are unhappy with the reduction in download time you have achieved, you can run the procedure again. However, Flash will reach a stage where it cannot remove any more curves and you will not be able to optimise further.

Further ideas

You will have noticed two other options which are also on the **Modify** drop-down menu. These are:

* **smooth**
* **straighten**.

Both of these tools reduce the amount of information needed to create an object and so may be seen as part of the process of optimising the shapes you create.

More on layers — setting the order

The layers you have used throughout this animation have been created so that they do not clash. However, as you create your own animation, you may find that the star of your animation has been hidden behind a tree or some other secondary object. How frustrating! Luckily, it is easy to sort this out; it is simply a case of changing the order of layers in the stack on the left-hand side of the timeline. Basically, the higher up the list, the nearer the contents are to you on the screen. You just need to remember that new layers automatically appear higher up than older ones.

To change a layer's position in the list, click on it and drag it to the new position.

Exporting for use on the web

When you have finished your animation, you will want to export it. Flash offers a range of options you could use to do this. Of these options, there are three on which it is best to concentrate. These include exporting as:

* a Flash file
* HTML
* a GIF.

Activity 15: Publishing your animation...

In this activity you will:

* learn about the different formats in which you could publish your completed animation.

▶ Select **File...Publish Settings**.

The **Publish settings dialogue box** will appear. This shows the eight different formats you could use to publish your animation, as well as the location to which the file will be published.

Each of the possible formats has an associated publish settings tab. When you select a format, the tab is added. If you deselect all possible formats, only the default Formats page will remain.

Once you have changed any settings, you can then select **Publish** from the bottom left-hand side of the dialogue box.

You need to understand the main formats you could use and how they differ. We will look at each in turn.

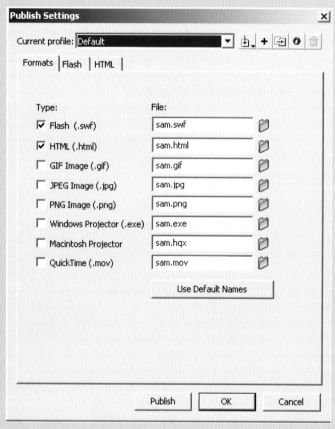

Figure 10.24: *Publish Settings dialogue box.*

Export as a Flash file

Flash files are exported as .SWF files, which stands for **Shockwave for Flash**. Flash files play on a **Flash Player**. This is a piece of software which needs to be on the computer of anyone who wants to view .SWF files. However, it is a safe bet that most people will now have this software on their computers.

There are a few publishing options of which you need to be aware:

● **Generate size report** – this is a report which shows the breakdown of the .SWF file and gives frame-by-frame analysis of the movie's size. This is very useful for optimising the animation.
● **Protect from import** – this stops anyone importing your .SWF file back into Flash and editing it. Unless you intend your work to be further developed by others, you should always check this option.
● **Compress movie** – this allows Flash to compress the animation on publication. This is a requirement of this unit, so it is probably a good idea to select this option!

Export as HTML

The single most obvious advantage of HTML is that it is the universal language of the Internet. When you publish your animation as an HTML file, your animation will be embedded within an HTML page. You can then edit this page to add other HTML elements. This makes this option a very simple and powerful option, if you know how to edit HTML or can use web page authoring software.

Options of which you need to be aware include:

- **Template** – this is where you set the sort of HTML file into which the .SWF file is embedded. For further information on each format, click the **Info…** button
- **Dimensions** – this is where you set the size of the .SWF as it appears on the screen. You can choose to match the size on the page to the size of the animation, or you choose to define either the pixel or percentage size of the file.
- **Playback options** – these are self explanatory. Before you choose which of these settings you will apply, check back on your original design plans.
- **Quality** – this sets the rendering quality at which your animation will play. This is especially useful if your animation is going to be viewed on slower computers. As you reduce the quality setting, the quicker the animation will run. You should use the **Auto High** option, as this allows Flash to change the quality of the animation if necessary.
- **Alignment** – there are two alignment options. **HTML alignment** chooses the alignment on the page, while **Flash alignment** sets where your animation will be within the player window.

Export as a GIF

Early web animation was based around animated GIFs. You will still find many examples of animated GIFs on the web. You may even have reviewed one for Assessment Objective 1.

One option of which you should be aware is:

- **Playback** – this allows you to choose whether you want to publish your animation as a static image or as an animated image. It would seem odd to create a static version of your animation, after all the work that has gone into it, so choose **animated**.

CHAPTER 11

→ *Assessment Objective 4*

Test the Animation

Overview:

Testing was discussed in Chapter 6 and you will need to go back to that section to review the discussion on why we test and how to present evidence of using a test table to plan and record testing.

How this assessment objective will be assessed...

You will need to provide evidence that you have planned and carried out at least four tests for a **Pass**, five for a **Merit** and six for a **Distinction**. You will also need to show that you have made changes to your animation as a result of what you discovered while testing. We hope to show that these changes are quite simple to make and that you should change most errors you discover.

Skills to use...

Good planning is the key to testing. It is very easy to miss one element off a test table and be penalised for it. As you create your animation, keep a note of any elements, transitions or effects which you apply. For higher level work, each and every element, transition and effect needs to be tested.

How to achieve...

Pass requirements

P1 You will test your animation using a test table with at least four tests.

P2 Most tests will be appropriate.

P3 You will identify areas for improvement.

Merit requirements

M1 You will test your animation using a test table with at least five tests.

M2 Tests will cover the main areas of the animation.

M3 You will identify areas for improvement and will make one necessary change suggested by the testing.

Distinction requirements

D1 You will test your animation using a test table with at least six tests.

D2 Tests will cover all main areas of the animation and will all be appropriate.

D3 You will identify areas for improvement and will make most changes suggested by the testing.

Testing

We discussed testing in Chapter 6. A lot of the concepts and ideas behind testing, as well as how to use a test table to record results, were discussed in that chapter. This chapter will concentrate on how you test your animation. If you want to review *why* we test, you should go back to Chapter 6.

What makes a test appropriate?

Basically, a good test is a test which tests something which needed to be tested, in a way which makes sense. A bad test either tests something which did not need to be tested, or tests something which needed to be tested but does so in a pointless way. Simply put, an inappropriate test is a waste of time. An appropriate test is not.

Activity 1: Suitable tests...

In this activity you will:

● identify suitable tests.

Below is a list of tests which may be applied to an animation. The animation will be run on a touch screen.

▶ Click on the button and see if the animation moves to the correct frame.

▶ Watch the video and check whether the main character is called Vince.

▶ Check whether the mouse moves the pointer over the main picture.

▶ Test how long the animation runs.

Which of these tests are appropriate and why?

What needs to be tested?

The syllabus identifies six areas which you need to test. These are:

1 suitability of content
2 delivery of message
3 frame rate
4 running time
5 correct looping
6 suitable file format.

We will now discuss how each area may be tested. Once you have completed your testing, you will need to make any necessary changes to your animation.

Suitability of content

It is very easy to launch into any project and get so excited that you forget to look at the big picture. In fact, you may become so excited by the superb animation that you forget that you have used a dummy photograph as one of your elements at the start of the project while you were waiting for the real ones to arrive, or that you made up a name for someone while you were trying to find out their real title. These mistakes and many more like them are very easy to make.

Your first test is really looking for that sort of mistake. It is also possible that you misinterpreted the target audience or purpose of the animation and have simply chosen an image or some other element which is totally inappropriate.

This test is best run by watching the completed animation. It could be done while watching individual frames or by manually moving through the animation using the **playhead**, but by watching the animation as it is intended to be seen, you can sometimes pick out some of the more subtle mistakes.

If you find unsuitable elements, they must be replaced with elements which are suitable. This sounds simple but may take a while!

An example of an inappropriate test would be to test the content against the needs of the wrong audience. If you think about it, this is what most of us do when we decide to include elements because *we* like them, rather than asking ourselves if the target audience would like them.

Delivery of message

This test is very much like the previous one, in that you are testing what you think is perfect, but which, because of your excitement and enthusiasm, may not be. In this test, you are simply checking that your aim has been met.

This test is also one which is best done by watching the completed animation, because only then will you be able to check on the whole product. As you watch, keep a clear idea of the aim of the animation in your head. If you feel that the animation does not meet this aim, then you need to be clear why not. This may be a matter of which images or graphics you have used, the sound or even the quality of your animation. It may even be possible that you have completed the animation exactly as you planned when using the storyboard, but that your original planning was wrong.

Frame rate

This test is a simple one. All you have to do is watch the animation. If the animation runs too quickly, then you probably have too many frames per second. Signs which show that your frame rate is too high include how quickly people are moving. If a character is supposed to be moving their legs as if they are walking, they should not be moving at running speed. Alternatively, if you have too low a frame rate, maybe five frames for example, what would take half a second to happen at a frame rate of ten frames per second takes a full second. Signs of this would be a feeling of slow motion on the screen. It may be funny but it is probably not the effect you want.

Luckily, this is an easy one to repair. If you open your animation in the Flash Authoring software, you can change the **Frame Rate** by changing the setting on the **document properties panel**.

TIP
Remember that if you change the frame rate of a presentation, you will change the time it takes for your presentation to run.

Running time

This could be another visual test. Get your stopwatch out and start the animation. Fifteen seconds? **Pass** criteria achieved! Thirty seconds, **Merit** or **Distinction** level. Brilliant!

Alternatively, you could divide the total amount of frames by the frame rate. The table below shows the relationship between **frames**, **frame rate** and **time**.

Amount of frames	6 frames per second	12 frames per second	24 frames per second
180	30 seconds	15 seconds	7.5 seconds
240	40 seconds	20 seconds	10 seconds
360	60 seconds	30 seconds	15 seconds
480	80 seconds	40 seconds	20 seconds

If you find that your running time is incorrect, you could:

- change the frame rate
- include more content
- change the length of animations.

You may get away with changing the frame rate but this will probably affect the quality of the animation. It is probably better to accept that you have underestimated and add some more content or change the length of animations.

Correct looping

This is the easiest of all the tests. Just watch the animation. If you have designed an animation which deliberately includes looping, you probably want to avoid the irritating jump as the animation shifts from the last frame back to the first. After all, the rest of your animation has been as smooth as you could possibly make it.

If you have used the on-screen rulers as you worked through Sam's animation, the ball which rolls to and fro across the screen should not jump as you move from **frame 180** to **frame 1**. However, if it does, you will need to edit the final **keyframe** of the animation so that the ball ends up as close as possible to where it starts in **frame 1**.

Suitable file format

Because Flash is designed to create animations for use on the Internet, if you have used the **Publish** tool to complete your animation, you will have chosen a format which runs on the web. However, remember what we said about the different possible file formats. If you have saved your Flash document as a .gif file, is the file animated? Does your design include an instruction about the format you should use? Maybe you were told not to use Flash as the client did not want to use a Flash player. It is unlikely but it is still possible.

As with all the tests here, this is simple enough to remedy if you find a problem. In this case, just go back into Flash and republish your Flash document in the correct format.

Testing and making changes

The tests we have highlighted above all seem pretty clear. In fact, they seem so clear and the remedies which each suggest are so straightforward, that we expect you are all thinking that there is no reason why you should not test and repair everything. Great! If you have planned your time well and have done your testing accurately, there is no reason why you should not make all necessary changes. After all, this is what happens in the real world.

Testing Sam's animation

You should now have a completed animation but there may be some elements which need improving. You need to test the animation following the steps we have explained above. You will need to construct a **test table** before you start your testing. Refer back to Chapter 6 in the web planning and creation chapters of this book for an explanation of how to create one.

As you test, remember to provide evidence. Where you have had to watch the animation in order to test it, notes taken during the test will be good evidence. For other tests, such as the **content test**, a list of elements on the animation, including the effects used as well as any transitions, with comments, will be good evidence.

You should also provide evidence of having made changes. Screenshots are the best way of showing changes. A screenshot of an image as it appears on a stage, with the new image which replaces it, is clear evidence that you have changed your animation as you have shown in your **test table**.

Appendix: Storyboard for Sam's Animation

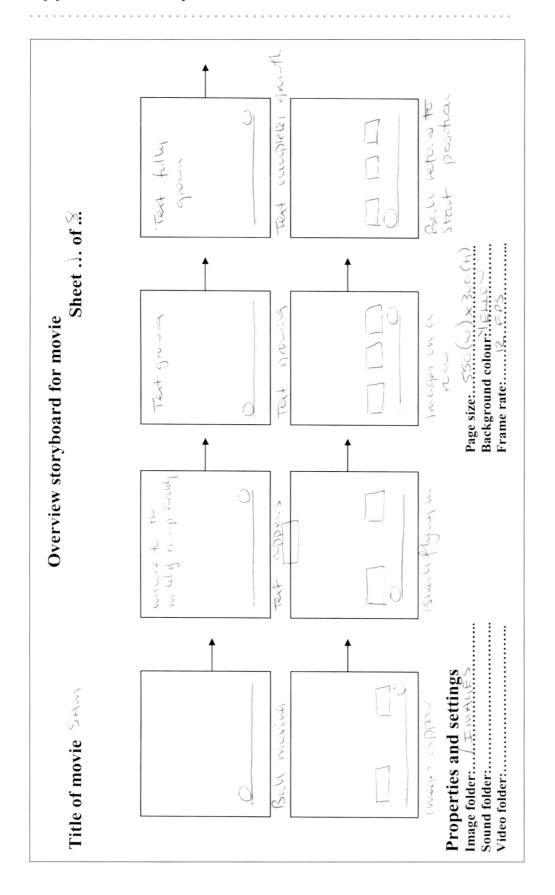

Overview storyboard for movie

Sheet .1. of .8.

Title of movie SAM

Back movie

Image capture / IMAGES

Welcome to the wildlife camp freely

Text appears

Sketch flying in

Text growing

Text growing

Image in a row

Text fully grown

Text completes growth

Back returns to start position

Page size: ...55c(w) x 3cc(h)

Background colour: ...Blue

Frame rate: ...12..FPS

Properties and settings

Image folder: ...IMAGES...

Sound folder: ......

Video folder: ......

Storyboard for movie

Title of movie Sam

Sheet 2 **of** 8

Start of section

Transition applied during section

Ball rolls along the line. Rotates few times in a clockwise direction.

Close of section

Components

Images: Line and ball on layers)
Sound None
Video None
Other None

Components

Images: Line and ball on layers
Sound None
Video None
Other None

Storyboard for movie

Title of movie Sam

Start of section

Small text

Transition applied during section

Ball rolls from right to left in a counter clockwise direction. Rolls four times.

Text appears at start of section and is still growing at the end of the section.

Close of section

Text growing but not complete

Components

Images: Link and Ball on layers
Sound ....
Video ....
Other Text ....

Components

Images: Link and Ball on layers
Sound ....
Video ....
Other Text "Welcome to the world of Camp Freddy"

Storyboard for movie

Sheet 4. of ...8

Title of movie

Start of section

Text growing but not complete

0

Close of section

Full size text

0

Transition applied during section

Bell → left - right, 4 times, clockwise.

Text completes it build by the time bell has moved to the far right.

Text will disappear off the screen at the end of animation.

Components

Images: live ones bell & text layers

Sound

Video

Other Text

Components

Images: live ones bell enlarges

Sound

Video

Other Text

Storyboard for movie

Sheet 5.. of ..8

Title of movie

Start of section

Transition applied during section

This is one frame on from the previous sheet. 2small.jpg and 3small.jpg appear. 1small.jpg begins movement along the motion path from off screen at top. By the time ball reaches LHS, 1small.jpg is half way through motion

Close of section

Components

Images: Line cner ball, 1small.jpg, 2small.jpg and 3small.jpg

Sound ....

Video ....

Other ....

Components

Images: Line cner ball, 1small.jpg, 2small.jpg & 3small.jpg

Sound ....

Video ....

Other ....

Storyboard for movie

Title of movie

Sheet 6 ... of 8 ...

Start of section

2small | 3small

Transition applied during section

1small.jpg completes the journey along motion path.

Ball rolls left to right, 4 revolutions clock wise.

Close of section

2small | 1small | 3small

Components

Images: 2small.jpg e 3small.jpg

Line cmd Ball, 4small jpg

....

Sound

....

Video

....

Other

....

Components

Line cmd Ball, 4small.jpg

Images: 2small.jpg cmd 3small.jpg

....

Sound

....

Video

....

Other

....

Storyboard for movie

Title of movie

Sheet ..7.. of ..8..

Start of section

Components

Images: Live cover Bell 1small.jpg 2small.jpg 3small.jpg

Sound ....

Video ....

Other ....

Transition applied during section

1small, 2small & 3small stay in place Bell moves along line from right to left, rotate & then counterclockwise.

Close of section

Components

Images: Live cover Bell, 1small .jpg 2small.jpg 3small.jpg

Sound ....

Video ....

Other ....

Storyboard for movie

Sheet .8. of .8.

Title of movie

Start of section

Close of section

Transition applied during section

Move loops back
to the beginning.

4small, 2small and
3small disappear
off the screen

Components

Images: Line and ball, 2small.jpg
2small.jpg and 3small.jpg

Sound ....

Video ....

Other ....

Components

Images: Line and ball on layers
....

Sound ....

Video ....

Other ....

Index